Empire in Brazil

Empire in Brazil

A NEW WORLD EXPERIMENT
WITH MONARCHY

C. H. HARING

The Norton Library
W · W · NORTON & COMPANY · INC ·
NEW YORK

Preface

Books in English on the history of Brazil, our largest and most populous Latin American neighbor, are remarkably few. This little volume — an expansion of eight public lectures delivered in Boston in November 1955 under the auspices of the Lowell Institute — is a slight effort to meet the deficiency. It is addressed to the general public — not a scholar's manual. It is not a contribution to knowledge in the sense of being based on an independent examination of documentary sources. It does reflect a wide reading of the best Brazilian historical works on the subject of the Braganza Empire. The appended bibliography is a list of the books consulted, and may serve as an *apologia* for the writer's venture.

The notes, kept to a minimum, are most of them a concession to the stray scholar who may happen upon these pages. The book as a whole is frankly lifted out of the contributions by Brazilian historians. Where interpretations differ, however, the writer has presented his own judgment based upon a life-long interest in Brazilian and Spanish American history in general. If this book creates a desire in the American reading public to know more about the great Brazilian nation, it will have accomplished its purpose.

Throughout the text, Portuguese words are spelled according to the official orthography now used in Brazil, but for books cited in notes and bibliography the spelling as it appears on the title page is preserved. On the map of Brazil, provincial boundaries appear as in the time of the Empire.

C. H. H.

Contents

Chapter One

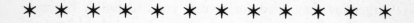

UNIQUENESS OF BRAZIL —

SECESSION FROM PORTUGAL

Among all the new-born nations of the American hemisphere in the nineteenth century, only Brazil was able successfully to preserve the institution of monarchy. From 1822, the year in which the Brazilians separated from the mother country, Portugal, until 1889, they were governed by emperors under a constitutional regime.

Brazilians were not alone in this desire to retain in the New World the institutions with which they had been familiar in the Old. Other Latin American communities in their struggle for independence harbored the idea of setting up a native or American monarchy. One actually made the experiment — Mexico — without success. Brazil alone accomplished it. In Chile, Argentina, and Peru many of the conservative, landowning class thought along similar lines. Most of them wanted political independence — that is, escape from the political, economic, and social inferiority imposed upon them by their colonial status. But many believed that monarchy was what the popular masses really understood and respected. To many it seemed to be the only guarantee of political and social stability. It would commend itself more readily to the monarchical governments of Europe whose diplomatic recognition they devoutly hoped for. It would also preserve the aristocratic framework of society with which their personal interests, economic and social, were identified.

In Chile and Peru the patriot leaders never got so far as to set up a king, or even to invite one to rule over them. In Argentina they tried for several years to find a European prince, and conceivably might have succeeded, had not the government in Buenos Aires been defeated and scattered by the presumably more democratic, rural, provincial forces in the interior.

The Mexicans, in default of a Spanish prince from Europe, accepted somewhat reluctantly one of their own number, Agustín de Iturbide, By Divine Grace First Emperor of the Mexicans. But he survived for only a year, 1822–23. One really couldn't accept or respect one's next-door neighbor as king or emperor, especially if he displayed more concern for the trappings of royalty than intelligent understanding of the critical problems facing a brand new nation. As for real princes — men who however unworthy they might be personally bore in the minds of their contemporaries the ineffable stamp of birth if not of breeding — they were not especially attracted by the prospect of rule over distant, unruly, half-Indian communities. It was in Brazil, and Brazil only, that after a revolt from the Portuguese crown, monarchy survived — largely because a prince of the ruling Portuguese dynasty happened to be at hand. And it endured until near the close of the nineteenth century.

In other ways Brazil was unique among the nations of Latin America. It is, first of all, a Portuguese-speaking nation — although many of our fellow citizens still confuse it with Spanish America — the only Portuguese nation in the Western Hemisphere. There are eighteen Spanish American nations.

It is, in fact, preëminent in the Portuguese world today, supplanting in many respects the parent country. Not only much greater in population and area than Portugal, but in literature, the fine arts, economic resources, industrial development, and promise for the future, Brazil today far outranks the old metropolis. Also among the nations of Latin America, Brazil is by far the largest in area, the most populous, and potentially the most powerful. In these respects it equals approximately all the rest of South America put together. With an Atlantic seaboard of some 3,700 miles, it is larger than the continental United States exclusive of Alaska, larger by some 250,000 square miles, or by an area the size of the state of Texas.[1]

Brazil repudiated Portuguese rule in 1822, when upper-class Brazilians decided that the time had come to fend for themselves as an independent nation. The masses, for the most part illiterate, were scarcely yet a segment of the body politic. A nationalistic sentiment, a feeling of separateness from Europe and Europeans, had been growing in Brazil for a long time. Brazilian historians carry it back at least to the middle of the seventeenth century, when the Dutch West India Company seized and held for a quarter-century the coastal area in the northeast around Pernambuco; just as contemporaneously they established themselves in North America in the valley of the Hudson River. These Dutch intruders were ultimately expelled from Brazil by the efforts, almost unaided, of the colonists themselves. And this achievement gave to the

[1] Brazil's only Latin American rival in these respects has been Argentina, approximately one-third the size of Brazil in territory and population. Argentina may possess an advantage in a citizenry of more purely European stock, but this is debatable. It is less richly endowed with mineral, forestal, and even potential agricultural resources than its Portuguese neighbor. And if, a generation ago, it was well in the lead in political stability, intellectual activity, and economic prosperity among the peoples of Latin America, these advantages were sacrificed in the political disaster of the Perón regime.

Portuguese Americans an enhanced sense of their own self-sufficiency, and some disillusionment perhaps with their Portuguese cousins in Europe.

On several occasions in the following century and a half there were armed conflicts between American-born and European-born Portuguese; protests usually against the privileged position occupied by the latter in government and trade, or against the social inferiority in which Americans were held by Europeans generally. There is no doubt that the example of the thirteen English continental colonies in achieving independence from Great Britain had considerable influence on the minds of contemporary Brazilians, as had the new concepts of liberty and equality released by the French Revolution. Cultural relations were intimate between Portugal and France, and the catastrophic course of events in Paris was followed closely by intellectual circles in Brazil. In short, the early years of the nineteenth century were a time of conflicting ideologies, of social turmoil and change, under any regime old or new. The parallel with our own age is obvious enough. And the Portuguese Brazilians, with their own special grievances, responded to the spirit of the times.

These forces were at work in all the American colonies, Spanish and Portuguese, and in both Portuguese and Spanish America the course of events culminating in political independence was occasioned and fashioned by the situation in Europe, more specifically by the seizure in 1807–08 of both Portugal and Spain by the armies of Napoleon Bonaparte. In Spanish America the effect was a bitter military struggle of some fifteen years' duration before independence of the continental colonies was finally achieved. In Brazil the course of events was very different. The first impulses to independence were in fact received from the Portuguese royal family itself.

When a French army under General Junot approached Lisbon near the end of November 1807, the royal family and the court fled overseas to Brazil under the protection of a British fleet. Portugal for a century had been to all intents and purposes an economic protectorate of England, and in the gigantic struggle then involving all of Europe, a choice had to be made between the military imperialism of Napoleon and the economic imperialism of Great Britain. At the Portuguese court there were sharply opposing currents, one English, the other French. In this painful dilemma, the Portuguese crown and its chief advisers, after last-minute hesitations, chose to remain loyal to their traditional allies. The sovereign at this time was Maria I, but she was insane, and the actual government was in the hands of her son and heir, the Prince Regent Dom João. When Junot approached the city gates, the royal flight had the appearance of a panic, but it evidently had been discussed and decided upon in detail, for treasure, archives, and all the apparatus of administration were on board the fleet when the hesitant Prince Regent finally embarked.

After a brief sojourn in the ancient city of Bahia, the exiles sailed on to Rio de Janeiro in March 1808. Rio became the temporary capital of the Portuguese Empire. As Oliveira Lima has remarked, the event was unique: the emigration of a European court overseas, the transfer across the Atlantic of the seat of one of the great empires of the Old World, an empire that still included, besides Brazil, the islands of Cape Verde, Madeira, and the Azores, the vast unexplored territories of Angola and Mozambique in Africa, and establishments in India, China, and Oceania.[2]

The change was a great boon to Brazil. The old mercantile monopolies of Portugal associated with colonialism were swept away. On the advice of the governor of Bahia, the Conde da Ponte, and of José da Silva Lisboa, devoted follower of Adam Smith and Brazil's most distinguished economist of

[2] Manuel de Oliveira Lima, *Formation historique de la nationalité brésilienne* (Paris, 1911), p. 127.

his time, Brazilian ports were immediately thrown open to the trade of all friendly nations—to the special advantage of England, it need scarcely be added, especially when a treaty of trade and navigation two years later gave British merchants tariff concessions greater than those accorded to Portugal itself.[3] The step in any case was inevitable, for trade with the metropolis occupied by French armies was impossible, and foreign commerce was essential to sustain what was now the head of the Empire.

A variety of other reforms in Brazilian economic and cultural life were sanctioned, freeing them from old colonial restrictions: promotion of communications by land and water between the widely separated population centers; some improvement of the administration of justice and taxation; establishment of the first bank, mercilessly exploited by the government, and of a naval academy and a college of medicine and surgery; opening of the royal library of 60,000 volumes to the public; establishment of a botanical garden, or garden of acclimatization, of especial interest to the Prince Regent, and visited by tourists today; even a printing press was acquired for the first time in Brazil, in the beginning for official use only, but the first step toward the emergence of a public press. Measures were at the same time taken for the improvement of agriculture. It was in this period that the production of coffee began to expand under royal protection, and in the Botanical Garden was introduced the cultivation of oriental tea.[4] A Brazilian iron industry had its beginnings at this time, as well as the production of textiles, which was to be Brazil's most important manufacture in the nineteenth century.

Rio de Janeiro especially prospered and grew rapidly. Many

[3] The treaty also included the right of British subjects to be tried by their own judges, and the promise to abolish the African slave trade with Brazil.

[4] Manuel de Oliveira Lima, *Dom João VI no Brasil* (Rio de Janeiro, 1908), I, 190–215.

foreigners were attracted to Brazil, scientists and technicians, often invited by the crown. The development of the fine arts was accelerated by the increase of urban life and the brilliance of court functions. The arrival of a mission of French artists in 1816, at the suggestion of the Conde da Barca, minister of João VI — painters, sculptors, architects and musicians — became the nucleus of the later Academy of Fine Arts. Facilities were accorded to distinguished foreign naturalists — botanists and zoologists — who traversed great stretches of this vast territory, and whose writings are classics in the history of Brazilian scientific literature: Martius, Spix, Auguste de St. Hilaire, Eschwege, Prince Max of Wied-Neuwied. Brazil, in short, no longer an exploited colony, became a convergence of European culture.[5]

But there was another side to the picture. With the crown came a host of exiled aristocrats, courtiers, officials, generals, hangers-on, who had lost their properties in Portugal, some fifteen thousand, it is said. Many of them arrogant, avaricious, they monopolized the offices and sinecures in the government. Rio de Janeiro, a squalid, unhealthy tropical city of 130,000 inhabitants, without waterworks or sewers, where daily life had been simple and uneventful, had suddenly to lodge and maintain a throng of strangers accustomed to a much more sophisticated existence. Even the housing of these newcomers was a problem, and many Brazilians were constrained to vacate their residences in Rio to make room for them. Discomforts and grumblings on both sides were inevitable. Taxation too was necessarily heavier, for now it was left to Brazil alone to

[5] *Ibid.*, I, 229–258. Karl Friedrich Philipp Martius and Johann Baptist von Spix were members of a Bavarian scientific mission that came out to Brazil in 1817 with the Archduchess Maria Leopoldina, daughter of the Emperor Francis I of Austria and bride of Dom Pedro de Alcântara, heir to the Portuguese crown. Among them was a Viennese artist, Thomas Ender, whose many drawings and water colors of Brazil have only in recent years received adequate appreciation in exhibitions and books.

support a royal court and an army. In earlier days the occupation of Brazil had never been a military one. It had been practically impossible for the metropolis to maintain a numerous garrison in the widely scattered overseas provinces, and such forces as there were had been mostly Brazilian, a well-organized system of local militia. So many of the native Americans were gradually alienated. A latent hostility between Creole and Portuguese, between American and European, was intensified. And it appeared even among army officers.

It was also in part a racial question, for most of the Brazilians, even of the upper class, were of mixed ancestry. The mingling of races had been a characteristic of Brazilian society from the early days of the colony. In the beginning, when European women were few, Indian women became the mothers of the children of the Portuguese adventurers. And very soon Negroes were brought in as slaves from Portuguese possessions across the Atlantic in west Africa. Negro slaves became very numerous on the plantations in the sugar-growing area of Pernambuco and Bahia, and far outnumbered the whites. The white planter, besides his white family, often had a numerous colored progeny as well, who were frequently treated as the sons of their father and sometimes were educated. The Portuguese, in fact, have displayed little or no aversion to the so-called colored races, biologically or socially. Racial prejudice of the sort common among Anglo-Saxons has never existed in Portuguese countries.

The consequence was that most Brazilians, to a slight or greater degree, were of mingled European and Indian or African extraction, and the racial complexion varied from one region to another. In Amazonia the prevailing element was Indian, in the pastoral area of the northeast and the interior provinces of Mato Grosso and Goiás it was *mameluco* (Indian and white), along the sugar-producing coast from Rio de Janeiro to Pernambuco and Paraíba and in the mining region of Minas Gerais it was Negro and mulatto, and south of Rio there was a mingling of all three races with an increasing predominance of the European. The Portuguese who followed the court to Brazil were inclined to look down upon these Americans as mere colonials, but also as Indian or African, and jealousy and hostility between them was only aggravated.

The Prince Regent and the court had been driven from Portugal by the onslaught of the armies of Napoleon. After the reconquest of the Iberian peninsula by the forces of the Duke of Wellington and the exile of Napoleon, the Portuguese royal government might have been expected to return to Lisbon. But Dom João elected to remain in Brazil, despite the urgings of Lord Strangford, the British minister, that he restore normalcy in the old country and rejoin the galaxy of restored sovereigns in Europe. Dom João liked Brazil. Indeed he seems to have fallen under the influence of his American environment to a degree surprising in a sovereign born to absolute rule. In correspondence with Thomas Jefferson, President of the United States, he alluded to the "well-founded liberal principles, religious as well as political, that we both possess," and to the "most perfect union and friendship which I hope will continue without interruption between the nations that occupy this new world." [6] Rio de Janeiro itself, before it was embellished with wide avenues, manicured beaches and ultra-modern skyscraper apartments, although less healthful than today, must with its incredible natural environment have possessed even greater fascination and charm.

The Brazilians, as might be anticipated, bitterly opposed Dom João's departure, for fear that they might lose all that they had gained by the presence of the crown. Indeed Dom João in December 1815, in order to normalize the situation in the eyes of the European sovereigns meeting at the Congress of Vienna, was persuaded to elevate the colony to formal and

[6] A. J. Lacombe, *Brazil: período nacional* (Mexico, 1956), p. 51.

legal equality with the mother country. In the following year the mad queen died, and the Prince became King as João VI of the "United Kingdom of Portugal, Brazil and the Algarve."[7] Meantime Portugal was administered by a Council of Regency presided over by the British minister, Sir Charles Stuart, while a British general, Marshal Beresford, was Commander in Chief of the Army. If the Brazilians feared that the King would return to Europe, the Portuguese in Europe were as profoundly discontented at seeming to remain an appendage of their former colony and under alien rule. Moreover the disappearance of the old colonial trade monopoly had grievously affected Portugal's economic prosperity. Commercial treaties following that with Great Britain in 1810 had induced an active correspondence of Brazil with Europe and the United States, and the balance of trade with Portugal, formerly very favorable to the metropolis, was sharply reversed. Here was a dangerous dichotomy which the crown was never able satisfactorily to resolve.

In America the most serious international problem of the reign of Dom João VI was a conflict with Buenos Aires over possession of the eastern bank of the Río de la Plata, a conflict from which ultimately emerged the Republic of Uruguay. It involved on the one hand territorial ambitions of Portugal in America that harked back to the sixteenth century; on the other, the aspiration of Buenos Aires to constitute itself the heir of the Spanish Viceroyalty of the Río de la Plata; and both crossed by the desire of the natives of the Banda Oriental for political autonomy, if not independence. It is an episode that will be more appropriately discussed in the following chapter.

A domestic conflict — the republican revolt in 1817 in the

---

[7] The Algarve, the southernmost province of Portugal, was the last to be conquered from the Moors, and its appearance in the royal title was only of historical significance.

province of Pernambuco — revealed the continued smoldering of discontent among native Brazilians, especially in the northern provinces which shared few of the benefits enjoyed by the capital. Swayed to some extent by the example of the United States and by the struggle for independence in the Spanish colonies, it was sparked by antagonisms between Portuguese and native officers of the garrison, resulting in personal encounters and assassinations. Masonic influences were also involved, but fundamentally the outbreak was an expression of a deep-seated regionalism that has always been an important factor in the history of Brazil. A secret society had existed since 1814 aiming at the establishment of a republican government, and early in 1817 it was forced prematurely to resort to arms. Envoys were sent to the United States and England to obtain material aid if not official recognition, but disciplined forces were promptly dispatched from Bahia under the Conde dos Arcos, and the revolt was suppressed without difficulty and with unnecessary harshness. Its leader, Domingos José Martins, and several of his followers were executed, and others were banished or imprisoned. But the episode remains today a patriotic landmark in the history of Brazilian independence.

As circumstances in Napoleonic Europe had started a course of events that culminated in the emergence of Brazil from its former colonial status, so it was again political developments in Europe that gave occasion for the complete separation of Brazil from the mother country.

The year 1820 was a time of political upheaval in southern Europe. In Spain, Portugal, Italy, and Greece there were armed protests against the monarchical absolutisms that prevailed generally after the fall of Napoleon. In Portugal the liberal elements, fired by the example of revolution in next-door Spain, irritated by their continued bondage to an "English" regency, demanded a constitution and the return of their king. Uprisings first in Oporto and later in Lisbon, during the temporary absence of Beresford in Brazil, forced the Regency to summon a national parliament or Cortes, which took steps to elaborate a modern democratic constitution, by which Brazilians were to be accorded representation in the parliament.

The liberal movement, although not anti-Brazilian in the beginning, with the continued postponement of the King's return became the medium of the pent-up resentments of the Portuguese. It soon appeared that the Portuguese liberals, once they had their king back and their own liberties secure, were determined to reduce the American realm to its former condition of an exploited dependency. In Brazil the news of these events of 1820 produced a profound repercussion. Both groups, the Portuguese and the native American, displayed strong sympathies with the revolution in Lisbon. The Portuguese courtiers felt no strong attraction to a liberal constitution, but were intensely interested in returning with the King to their estates in Europe. The Brazilians hailed the constitution, but wanted to retain their king. Many preferred separate constitutions for the two kingdoms under the same crown, i.e., home rule for Brazil. And so there were demonstrations in all the principal cities, while in some of the provinces liberal juntas were chosen to replace the old captains general.

Dom João, well-meaning but temperamentally timorous and irresolute, knew not which way to turn. He was an old man, who by education and inheritance possessed little understanding of the constitutionalism fashionable at that time. But if he returned to Portugal, it was clear enough that he might lose Brazil. If he remained in Brazil, he would certainly lose Portugal. Meantime, although some representative Brazilians appeared in the Lisbon assembly and eloquently upheld their cause, all attempts at conciliation failed. The new constitution sharply repudiated the system of dual monarchy devised by Dom João VI.

In February 1821, the King, pressed by the Portuguese about him and by his son, the Crown Prince Dom Pedro, and threatened by mutiny in the garrison at Rio, issued a decree approving the Portuguese constitution (although it was unfinished and its exact terms were unknown), and a fortnight later announced his approaching departure. The British government threw its influence on the side of departure, and even prepared to send a squadron to Rio to convey him back to Europe.

Dom João also summoned Brazilian electors to a meeting in Rio to choose deputies to the Cortes in Lisbon. This assembly met on April 21, but it immediately proceeded, *ultra vires*, to announce a separate constitution for Brazil — the celebrated Spanish Constitution of 1812 — and to insist on the King's remaining in Brazil. These decisions the King, who so far had clutched at any pretense to avert the dreaded voyage back to Portugal, accepted next day. However on the following day the military stepped in, dispersed the assembly, and forced the unhappy monarch to reproclaim the Portuguese constitution. To complete the confusion, some believe that Dom João was himself privy to the whole stratagem. At any rate, on April 24 he boarded a warship and two days later sailed for Europe, taking with him most of the cash in the Bank of Brazil and all the jewels he could collect, and accompanied, it is said, by some three thousand of the Portuguese party. He left behind his son and heir, Dom Pedro, as regent in his place. In a famous letter addressed to Dom Pedro he anticipated the secession of Brazil, and advised him to take the crown for himself before some adventurer seized it.

Dom João VI was a genial, democratic, if rather weak and vacillating autocrat, but in general his government was enlightened and liberal. Although born to rule as an absolute sovereign, he was tolerant, clairvoyant, and fortunate in his choice of ministers. He "had the rare quality of being able to discover merit, and the rarer quality of not being jealous." [8] He left Brazil with regret, and Brazilians remember him with affection and gratitude as the ruler who, by raising Brazil out of its colonial abasement, made national independence inevitable.

A peculiar role was played in these episodes by the Crown Prince Dom Pedro, then twenty-four years of age. He was the favorite son of his father, to whom he was generally devoted, but of very different personality. Ardent, impulsive, courageous, with considerable native intelligence but with little formal education, he liked to identify himself with the liberalism then current. But temperamentally he was a child of eighteenth-century absolutism. In the incidents of February and April 1821, he is suspected of complicity with the Portuguese party in forcing the King's departure, although it was contrary to the desires of the Brazilian liberals. He was ambitious to remain behind as regent, as actually transpired. In fact, there is considerable evidence that Dom João VI had an understanding with his son that continued to the day of the King's death in 1826: that the only way the House of Braganza could retain control of the two countries was by Brazilian secession under Dom Pedro's leadership, with the expectation that the latter, retaining his right of succession in Portugal, would ultimately reunite the two crowns.

Thereafter events moved rapidly, impelled by the actions of the Cortes in Lisbon, which increasingly betrayed the intentions of even the liberals in Portugal to subject Brazil to its former colonial bondage. Decrees were issued abolishing the organs of central government at Rio and making the provinces individually responsible to Lisbon, with the obvious

[8] Oliveira Lima, *Formation historique*, p. 137.

intention of playing upon interprovincial jealousies and rivalries and preventing unity of action among the Brazilians. Another decree peremptorily ordered Dom Pedro to return at once to Portugal and prepare for a tour of Europe to complete his political education. At the same time Brazilians were by edict excluded from political and military offices. Dom Pedro in letters to his father noted the universal popular discontent, the profound agitation throughout the country, and the danger that extremists would conspire to establish a republic whether he was present or not.[9] In Portugal the old King, completely intimidated by the liberals, spied upon, in fear of his life, his correspondence violated, gave way to their least demands.

The instructions from Lisbon Dom Pedro, after some hesitation, refused to honor. And on January 9, 1822, in response to memorials and petitions from the provinces of São Paulo and Minas Gerais and from the Municipality of Rio de Janeiro urging him to remain with them in Brazil, he gave his celebrated promise: "As it is for the good of all and the general felicity of the nation, say to the people that I will remain." This is the famous *Fico* of Brazilian annals. It was a formal, public rejection of Portuguese authority and avowal of alliance with the American patriots, "the turning of a page in Brazilian history."

Two days later the Portuguese garrison in Rio retorted by demanding the Regent's compliance with the orders from the Cortes and threatening to bombard the city. Citizens and militia rushed to arms. The Portuguese commander, intimidated by the crowd, capitulated next day and moved the regiments across the bay to Niteroi. And a month later, for a price, he sailed with the garrison back to Europe.

At the same time Dom Pedro called into a newly formed Council of Ministers perhaps the most distinguished Brazilian

[9] João Pandiá Calógeras, *Formação histórica do Brasil* (São Paulo, 1938), p. 26.

of his day, José Bonifácio de Andrada. José Bonifácio was a native of São Paulo. He had studied at the Portuguese University of Coimbra and with eminent scientists elsewhere in Europe and had become a scholar and mineralogist of note. He lived for many years in Portugal where he held important official positions. He was a professor at Coimbra, perpetual secretary of the Academy of Sciences in Lisbon, and a member of many other European learned societies. He returned to Brazil in 1819 and soon rose to be the political leader of his native province. Early in 1822 he came to Rio de Janeiro to urge Dom Pedro to defy the Portuguese parliament and remained to be his chief minister. And it was his experience, energy, and statesmanship that guided the last steps to independence.

As remarked above, events moved rapidly. In February 1822 Dom Pedro published a decree creating a consultative council or junta to consist of representatives of all the provinces. In May he accepted from the Municipality of Rio the title, "Perpetual and Constitutional Defender of Brazil." In June he issued a call for a constituent assembly for Brazil in order to "establish the bases on which should be erected its independence." In August, in a series of proclamations, he urged the people to resist coercion, forbade the landing of Portuguese troops without his permission, and addressed a circular to the diplomatic corps announcing that Brazil was almost ready to proclaim its independence under the Braganzas. The final step was taken on September 7. While on a journey through São Paulo to unify resistance in that province, as he had already done successfully in the province of Minas Gerais, Dom Pedro was overtaken near a small stream called Ipiranga by a messenger from the Council in Rio with the latest Portuguese dispatches. The Cortes had revoked as rebellious the orders for the assembly of representatives of the provinces, had annulled all the acts of the Regent, and declared his ministers guilty of treason. There also arrived letters from his wife, the Princess Leopoldina, and from José Bonifácio insisting that the decisive moment had come.

Dom Pedro read the dispatches, and before his escort and with show of great indignation, crumpled them and ground them under his heel, drew his sword, and cried out, "The hour has come! Independence or death! We have separated from Portugal!" This was the famous "Cry of Ipiranga" of Brazilian history. There was no official act confirming this gesture. In fact, several earlier dates, in January, May, June, and August, were almost equally significant. But September 7 remains the Independence Day for all Brazilians.

Chapter Two

✳ ✳ ✳ ✳ ✳ ✳ ✳ ✳ ✳ ✳ ✳

THE PORTUGUESE LEGACY
DOM PEDRO I

The Cry of Ipiranga, the dramatic gesture of the Prince Regent proclaiming the separation of Brazil from its parent Portugal, was echoed with enthusiasm throughout the southern provinces. When the Prince appeared in Rio de Janeiro toward the end of the same month, September, he was received with a tremendous popular ovation. The Municipal Council of Rio declared its intention to make him constitutional emperor. Dom Pedro formally assented on October 12, and on December 1 he was solemnly crowned as Dom Pedro I, Emperor of Brazil. The ceremony was on a grand scale, with ritual borrowed from the coronation of Napoleon Bonaparte, of whom Dom Pedro was an ardent admirer. In fact, he was Napoleon's brother-in-law, for his wife, the Austrian Princess Leopoldina, daughter of the Austrian Emperor, was a sister of the French Empress Marie Louise.

Dom Pedro I ruled for nine years, until 1831 — a short, agitated reign. He was described by contemporaries as of medium height, with restless, brilliant black eyes and a face strongly marked by smallpox and partly covered by a magnificent black beard; a man who laughed easily and "liked to give a jovial tone to the most serious questions." He was a strange compound of good and bad qualities. He had natural ability, was ambitious, jealous of his authority, but was deficient in education and in political experience. He had been allowed to grow up among the servants and stableboys of the palace and found among them his boon companions. Yet he was not the uncultivated boor that some historians would make out. He apparently read and spoke French, translated English, and understood German (his wife was German). And he had a special fondness for Latin, or at least for the *Aeneid* and liked to quote from it on every occasion. He wrote verse with some ease, and was passionately fond of music, played several instruments, and revealed some talent as a composer. Most of the music played in the imperial chapel, we are told by a visiting Frenchman, was of his composing, to say nothing of the marches played in the parades of the imperial troops. But Dom Pedro's great delight was in outdoor exercise, for he was a man of splendid physique, incredible endurance, and like his imperial contemporary, the ill-fated Iturbide of Mexico, a superb horseman.[1]

On the other hand, he was impulsive, capricious, stubborn, a bundle of nerves, never in the best of health; capable of extremes of heroism and generosity and on occasion of the exact opposite; and was frank to the point of rudeness.[2] He had the desire to do the right thing, but with his undisciplined mind was not always able to accomplish it. "He was really liberal, in the exact sense of the word; but brought up in an absolutist environment, he did not always know how to demonstrate his liberalism, and at times was embarrassed in the choice between autocratic impulses and constitutional norms."[3]

[1] Sérgio Corrêa da Costa, *As Quatro corôas de D. Pedro I* [São Paulo, 1941], pp. 106–133.
[2] Calógeras, *Formação histórica*, p. 123.
[3] *Ibid.*, p. 124.

Fortunately the young Emperor had at his side as chief adviser and mentor, a scholar and statesman, José Bonifácio de Andrada. José Bonifácio was apparently convinced very early that secession was inevitable if Brazil was to retain its autonomy, but he was also a conservative, shocked by the excesses of the French Revolution of which he had been a witness in Europe. And so he prepared skillfully for independence under a constitutional monarchy, anticipating the more radical tendencies which, as actually happened in the Spanish colonies, might have swept the nation into a new-fangled republicanism.

Brazil had proclaimed itself a united independent empire. But real unity was still far from achievement. The revolt had been confined to four southern provinces, Rio de Janeiro, São Paulo, Minas Gerais, and Rio Grande do Sul. Portuguese reactionaries were numerous even there — rich merchants, landed proprietors, magistrates, and military officers. In several of the northern provinces, Bahia, Maranhão, and Pará, the Portuguese party still retained the ascendency, and Bahia's capital, Salvador, was occupied by a Portuguese garrison. The immediate problem, therefore, was the expulsion of the enemy from these areas. Given the immense distances, this could be accomplished only by sea, and José Bonifácio ordered the Brazilian chargé d'affaires in London to recruit sailors and officers. Through his agent in Buenos Aires he succeeded in obtaining the services of the renowned British admiral, Lord Cochrane, Earl of Dundonald, who had been campaigning for the Chileans against the Spaniards in the Pacific, but had fallen out with his employers. He now entered the service of Brazil to improvise a navy and drive out the remaining Portuguese forces.

Lord Cochrane was eminently successful, in a campaign still studied in the Naval War College at Rio de Janeiro as a strategic masterpiece. After an indecisive engagement with a superior Portuguese squadron at Bahia, he blockaded the port in May 1823, and aided by enveloping forces on land, compelled the enemy, ships and garrison, to evacuate early in July, taking with them the greater number of the Portuguese merchants. In hot pursuit, Cochrane's flagship found itself alone amid the Portuguese fleet, but such was the terror inspired by the admiral's repute, says Armitage, that they allowed him to capture a number of prizes virtually without combat. Learning that some of the transports were to sail for Maranhão and the rest to rendezvous at the island of Fernando de Noronha, he set sail for Maranhão, leaving Captain Taylor with a single ship, the *Niteroi*, to shadow the Portuguese to the mouth of the River Tagus, taking more prizes on the way. At São Luiz de Maranhão, Cochrane found several transports already arrived, but the local authorities immediately gave up the city, and the Portuguese troops were eventually permitted to continue on to Lisbon. Cochrane seized all the Portuguese shipping in the harbor and ordered the confiscation of all Portuguese properties. Only in the extreme north, in Belém do Pará, did the secessionist movement take a republican turn. So from Maranhão, Captain Grenfell was dispatched with the brig *Dom Miguel* and ninety-six men to occupy the city. Appearing before Belém, he obtained its surrender by leaving the impression that Cochrane with a strong force was at the river's mouth to overwhelm any resistance.[4]

Lord Cochrane finally departed from Maranhão in September 1823, arriving at Rio on November 9 where the Emperor conferred on him the title of Marquis of Maranhão. It had been chiefly by his efforts that the territory of Brazil was cleared of the enemy. There remained only the disputed area in the extreme south, Montevideo and the eastern bank of the Río de la Plata, which had been formally annexed by forces

---

[4] John Armitage, *The History of Brazil . . . 1808 . . . 1831* (London, 1836), I, 99–107. For the story of an attempted revolt in the city, its suppression by Grenfell, and the frightful aftermath, see *ibid.*, pp. 107–108.

from Brazil in 1821, the year before the emergence of the Empire. When the news of independence arrived, Portuguese and Brazilian troops there came to blows, until the former, after enduring a siege of seventeen months in Montevideo, abandoned the city on orders from the Portuguese Cortes.

By January 1824 the political unity of Brazil was accomplished. In those early days, however, there was little genuine unity in organization or spirit. The country was vast, its coastline extremely long, much of its interior difficult of access, its population of four and a half millions concentrated on a narrow coastal belt. There had been little unity in colonial times. Areas of settlement were widely separated; overland communications were difficult and very primitive, mostly by rivers or mule trails. Some of the provinces or "captaincies," especially Maranhão and Pará north of the "bulge," had until the nineteenth century been independent of the viceroy or other central authority in the south, and subject directly to the metropolis.[5] The Portuguese crown, in fact, had never been interested in Brazilian administrative unity, only in government that facilitated the collection of revenues. The captaincies were regarded as quite separate entities and generally treated as distinct administrative problems reflecting local peculiarities; a pragmatic policy that had engendered a regional, particularist spirit that was never more apparent than at the moment of independence, whether among the Brazilian deputies in the Portuguese Cortes or in Brazil itself.

Moreover, an old jealousy survived between the provinces

[5] With the settlement of the extreme north in the early years of the seventeenth century, and because of the difficulty of sailing from north to south against contrary winds and currents, the area from Ceará to Amazonas was in 1621 organized as the "State of Maranhão" (after 1774 two states of Maranhão and Grão Pará), independent of the older area farther south known thereafter specifically as the "State of Brazil." Hence the divergent tendencies in that area, more inclined to loyalty to Portugal, and the need of Lord Cochrane's fleet to bring these provinces into line.

of the northeast, dominated by Bahia and Pernambuco, and the southern provinces led by São Paulo and Rio de Janeiro. For two centuries, while cane sugar was the prime export to Europe and the wealth and ostentation of the planters of Pernambuco and Alagoas were of international notoriety, Salvador, capital of Bahia, was the seat of central government. But in the eighteenth century, with the decline of the sugar industry in competition with the West Indian islands, and the meteoric rise of gold and diamond mining in the region of Minas Gerais (General Mines) behind Rio de Janeiro, the capital of Brazil in 1763 was shifted to Rio, where it has remained ever since. But Bahia did not forget its former pre-eminence, and when the Portuguese Regent and his court, flying before the armies of Napoleon, tarried at Bahia in January 1808, its inhabitants had hoped to persuade them to remain.

The new Empire therefore was really an aggregation of nearly twenty scattered, centrifugal provinces, many of them with a tradition of autonomy or independence, held together by the prestige of the Braganza dynasty. A truly nationalist sentiment had still to be created. The role of Dom Pedro was expected to be that of reconcilor, mediator, between the north and the south, between the Portuguese and the Brazilian, between the old and the new. Indeed, except for the presence of the Emperor, Brazil might have gone the way of the Spanish empire in America where the territorial and administrative divisions flew apart to form a galaxy of separate and independent republics. The ruling class among the Brazilians, the planters and professional men, were most of them conservatives, who would have remained faithful to the union with Portugal had the latter shown any signs of respecting the autonomy of their country. But with the choice of secession imposed upon them, they preferred to avoid dangerous innovations in government, and accepted "monarchy as the only formula of national unity"; preferred it also as the system to which the people at large were accustomed, rather than create a new order for which they were unprepared. Happily they had a prince of their own at hand. And of all the Latin American nations in the nineteenth century, Brazil remained politically the most stable. A revolution in the national government occurred only once, in 1889, when monarchy was believed by many to have outlived its usefulness, and a federal republic was substituted. And like the revolution of 1822, it was almost bloodless.

The first important task of national consolidation was to draft a constitution, and the National Assembly summoned for this purpose in June 1822 met in Rio de Janeiro the following April, while Admiral Cochrane was preparing to drive the Portuguese from the northern provinces. It included among its number, it must be said, the cream of the nation: lawyers, clergy, landed proprietors, military officers. Most of the principal political figures of the first half-century of the Empire were members of this first Brazilian congress. A committee was appointed which proceeded to formulate a constitution not unlike the Charter of the Restoration Monarchy in France. But the Assembly soon revealed its political and parliamentary inexperience, soon indulged in vigorous anti-Portuguese and even in what sounded like antimonarchical sentiments. And José Bonifácio himself, deputy from São Paulo as well as Minister of State speaking for the government, did not possess the amiable and conciliatory personal qualities needed in a parliamentary leader to guide the group and help resolve its difficulties.

Republican ideas had taken some root in Brazil since the achievement of independence by the United States, and also federalist notions in provinces that under Portugal had been as separate from one another as the North American English colonies. Both concepts were advanced in the debates in the Assembly, although in the end the unitary system prevailed as more compatible with monarchy. The most critical issue was that of the Portuguese, and the most delicate. For there were many Portuguese in the country who had chosen to throw in their lot with Brazil. Some had rendered yeoman service in the cause of independence, and held important positions under the crown. Some of the imperial ministers, and almost all the palace officials, were Portuguese; and of more concern, many of the army officers were of Portuguese birth. The Emperor himself, of course, was a Portuguese. This situation disturbed many members of the Assembly, and some demanded that all Portuguese who did not appear to be wholly devoted to independence and constitutionalism be expelled from the country.

José Bonifácio had two distinguished brothers, Antônio Carlos and Martim Francisco. The former was the ablest orator of his day, the other was Minister of Finance. Both were members of the Assembly, and both were involved in these anti-Portuguese demonstrations. At the same time, many of the more radically minded Brazilians were impatient of José Bonifácio's essentially conservative policies. Among them was a group that had been in the forefront of the independence movement, but were jealous of his ascendency with the Emperor and intrigued to supplant him, and their center of activity was in the Masonic lodges.

Freemasonry had been introduced into Brazil in late colonial times, and ever since the departure of Dom João VI the Masonic lodges had been the focus of secessionist zeal. They dominated the Municipal Council of Rio de Janeiro, and at every forward step disputed with the Minister of State his leadership and initiative. José Bonifácio himself was a Mason and for a

short time was Grand Master, but in the bitter rivalry with
this group he even induced Dom Pedro in November 1822 to
suppress the lodges and exile their leaders.[6]

At the other extreme were wealthy reactionaries, merchants
and planters, who hated José Bonifácio because of his advanced ideas of social and economic amelioration: abolition
of the slave trade, a big business in Brazil; breakup of the great
landed estates; raising of the living standards of the laboring
classes. And finally there were the temperamental shortcomings of José Bonifácio himself. True humility was never a dis-
tinguishing trait of any of the Andrada clan. José Bonifácio,
secure in his intellectual superiority and worldly experience,
was often arrogant or ironical toward others, intolerant, impatient of opposition, overvigorous perhaps in his repressive
measures against those he believed hostile to the new government. All of which added up to a growing resentment against
the crown's chief adviser. Courtiers insisted to the young Emperor that he free himself from a despotic tutelage to this
arrogant, overbearing old man.[7] And although relations between Emperor and minister had always been cordial, almost
as those between father and son, these insinuations ultimately
had their effect.

Dom Pedro himself was beginning to feel his oats, and to
believe that he was the hero of Brazilian independence, that he

[6] José Bonifácio had been elected Grand Master on May 28, and later
proposed the Prince Regent as a member. But on August 20, in his absence,
his foes in the Gran Oriente made Dom Pedro Grand Master in his place.
In October he persuaded the Regent to suspend the lodges until further
order, and when the latter reversed his decision later in the month, he
resigned, only to be recalled within three days in response to popular clamor.
The vengeance of the irascible José Bonifácio was rapid and energetic. The
Masonic Order was again suspended, and its sponsors arrested or deported —
"poor beginning of the constitutional regime," its historian remarks. O. T.
de Sousa, *José Bonifacio emancipador del Brasil* (Mexico, 1945), pp. 145,
155, 165, 177–183.

[7] Their intrigues may also have been abetted by the interested influence of
Dom Pedro's mistress, the later Marquesa de Santos.

had transformed the Brazilian colony into a vast empire. And so, in July 1823, by issuing a series of decrees annulling many of the police measures of his minister, he brought about José Bonifácio's resignation and that of his brother, Martim Francisco, the able Minister of Finance. It was a momentous step in the history of Brazil, for José Bonifácio was the real creator of the Brazilian Empire, the one person who guided the inexperienced and volatile prince in the straight and narrow, and whose continued presence at the Emperor's side might have averted some of Dom Pedro's egregious mistakes.

In the following September the special committee presented to the Assembly its projected constitution, creating a representative system of government in accord with the best liberal constitutional models of the time. But in the debates that followed, nationalistic, anti-Portuguese sentiments flamed up anew, both in the Assembly and in the public press. Two newspapers were especially violent, *O Tamoio* and *Sentinela da Liberdade*, both of which were believed to be controlled by the Andradas and to reflect their views. Meantime the impression gained ground that "the Portuguese element, rich, powerful and influential . . . was attempting to exert anew its former preponderance, insinuating itself everywhere, in trade, in the highest posts of public administration, in the armed forces, in the government, in the most intimate circles and even among the personal attendants of the Emperor." [8]

The arrival from Portugal of emissaries with proposals aimed at the reunion of the two kingdoms did not serve to tranquilize passions. With an assault by two Portuguese military officers upon an innocent civilian believed to be the author of diatribes against the army in the press, the anti-Portuguese campaign rose to white heat, led by the three Andrada brothers. The situation became intolerable. The entire ministry resigned, whereupon the Emperor appointed a new min-

[8] Sousa, *José Bonifacio*, p. 209.

istry even more Portuguese and reactionary in complexion. Upon the continued intransigence of the opposition, Dom Pedro on November 11 dissolved the Assembly. Besieged by imperial troops for some twenty-seven hours, the deputies were eventually forced to disperse. José Bonifácio, his brothers, and other leaders were put under military arrest, and a week later boarded ship with their families for exile to Europe. As Oliveira Lima has remarked, Dom Pedro, romantically enamored of only a rhetorical constitutionalism, was really the victim of his family and temperamental inheritance.

The Emperor promised to convoke another constituent congress to work on a draft he himself would present, "a draft twice as liberal." Instead, he appointed a commission of his own, ten men wisely chosen,[9] be it said, to frame a new instrument of government. This constitution, after formal reference to the principal municipalities for approval, was imposed upon the nation by imperial proclamation in March 1824. It lasted for sixty-five years, until the fall of the monarchy in 1889.

The Constitution of 1824 did not differ materially from that proposed by the nation's deputies the year before, except that the balance of power in the government rested more clearly in the Emperor, rather than in the nation in congress assembled. It included the usual individual guarantees: freedom of religion,[10] of the press, and of speech, inviolability of property, and equality before the law. It provided for a Parliament or General Assembly of two houses: a Chamber of Deputies elected for a term of four years, and a Senate whose members were appointed for life by the Emperor from lists of three nominated by electors in each province. In both houses representation was on the basis of population. There

[9] Seven of the ten had been members of the National Assembly.
[10] Although non-Catholics might hold services only in buildings without the outward signs of a church.

was to be a responsible ministry, although the terms were somewhat ambiguous, an independent judiciary, and limited manhood suffrage.

It was in fact a vigorously centralized constitution. In the Emperor was concentrated a comprehensive authority called the Moderating Power. He had a suspensory veto over legislation and the right to dissolve or summon the Parliament at will. He chose not only the senators but also the ministers, the bishops, and the provincial "presidents" or governors. He was given the power of pardon and of revising judicial sentences. Provision was made for the election of provincial councils, but they received little or no administrative or political authority. On the contrary, through his ministers the Emperor might exert a preponderant influence upon local government. Through them he could control the appointment of local judges and chiefs of police, annul municipal elections, suspend magistrates and the resolutions of the provincial councils.[11]

It was not an inappropriate constitution for a country 90 per cent illiterate, with a population of perhaps four million, and an agricultural economy based on great landed estates and Negro slavery. The liberal agitation that resulted in political independence was the work of a zealous minority, scions of wealthy or prominent families who had studied at Coimbra and other European universities, exposed to the new philosophical and political ideas of the age, and who were to assume direction of the embryonic and widely dispersed nation. A principal problem was the creation of a strong central authority that would assure national unity and preserve Portuguese America from the demagoguery and tumult of its Spanish neighbors.

There was one important difference, however, in the minds

[11] F. J. de Oliveira Vianna, *Evolução do povo brasileiro* (São Paulo, 1923), pp. 211–242.

of Brazilians, between the Constitution of 1824 and that drawn up by the ill-starred Assembly. In the latter a sovereign people had delegated powers to the crown. In the former a sovereign prince of his imperial benevolence granted a constitution to his subjects, even though it was disguised by reference for approbation to the municipal councils. The upshot was a republican revolt in the same year, and again as in 1817 in Pernambuco. The refusal to submit to a provincial president appointed as a mere delegate of the central power set off a chain reaction. The Câmara or Municipal Council of Recife, which had been disposed to acquiesce in the Constitution presented by the Emperor, was turned out for another that vehemently repudiated it and in its place proclaimed the "Confederation of the Equator." Appeals to the northern provinces of Paraíba, Rio Grande do Norte, and Ceará to join forces with it met with little effective response, and imperial troops, supported by Lord Cochrane's ships, soon took possession of Recife. The movement collapsed, with the usual aftermath of executions and cruel repression.

The Pernambuco rebellion was the materialization of several things: the vibrant regionalism of the north, whose deputies in the Assembly had been the most fervent defenders of federalism and democracy; exasperation over the Emperor's cavalier treatment of the nation's representatives in congress; protest against the Moderating Power as a threat to the nation's freedom and independence, and against the life-term Senate as an attempt to create a Brazilian aristocracy; and a revival of the republican sentiment expressed in the earlier revolt of 1817. National confidence in the monarchy, shaken by these events, was not easily restored. The Emperor had presented the people with a constitution in whose liberalism he felt great pride, but he made little effort to abide by it. He chose and dismissed his ministers at pleasure, ignoring the susceptibilities of the national Parliament, and almost invariably from among his personal friends and associates, most of them marquises and viscounts of his creation. The ministers in turn as a rule studiously ignored the legislature. In fact, no Parliament was convoked until 1826, and although it met regularly thereafter, the Emperor gave little heed to its wishes. Dom Pedro came more and more to regard any criticism of his acts or of his personal authority as an attack on the dynasty. "The Crown was untouchable, the monarchy infallible."

Moreover, the Portuguese question remained, to irritate Emperor and subjects. Dom Pedro continued to surround himself with Portuguese advisers and military officers. The few Brazilians were ultra-royalists who for motives personal or otherwise played up to his absolutist proclivities. And so an opposition soon appeared, some of whom were of the extreme left, republicans influenced by the example of the United States. Others, of the center, were moderate monarchists who wanted a responsible parliamentary government like that of England. Supporting the Emperor was the extreme right, conservatives who were either absolutists or merely content with things as they were. From 1826 onward, the Chamber of Deputies was fairly consistently controlled by the opposition, which as time went on became more and more vocal. "The liberal experiment was not easy in a country without a parliamentary tradition, with a sovereign convincedly democratic but temperamentally authoritarian. Nor did the opposition know how to distinguish political interpellation from personal attacks, or the ministers fail to consider themselves humiliated by the necessity of presenting accounts and furnishing explanations." [12]

Another cause of discontent lay in the foreign policies of

[12] Lacombe, *Brasil: período nacional*, p. 71.

the reign, especially relations with Portugal. Dom João VI, after long and difficult negotiations, under pressure from Great Britain, recognized the independence of Brazil by treaty in August 1825.[13] To save face, he assumed *pro forma* the title of Honorary Emperor of Brazil and then resigned it in favor of his son. In the ratification of the treaty, he also declared that Dom Pedro remained the heir to the Portuguese throne, expressly excluding his younger son, Dom Miguel. In return, by a secret article, Dom Pedro undertook that the Brazilian government would be responsible for a debt of £1,400,000 owed by Portugal to Great Britain, and would also pay Dom João £600,000 for the palaces and other royal properties left in Brazil. This neat family arrangement greatly angered the Brazilians. They alone by their valor and determination had achieved their independence. They owed nothing to the King of Portugal, least of all a £2,000,000 indemnity. And in the first session of the new Parliament it provoked the demand that the nation's representatives share in the ratification of all foreign treaties.

What was more, in the following year Dom João VI died, and a regency acknowledged the heir presumptive, Dom Pedro, as Dom Pedro IV of Portugal. The Emperor now faced the same dilemma as had his father five years earlier. He would not be accepted as king by the Portuguese people unless he returned to Lisbon, but if he did so he would most certainly lose Brazil, especially as the Constitution of 1824 forbade Brazil to ally itself with any other nation by bonds of union or federation. He resolved the dilemma by reluctantly conceding the Portuguese crown to his daughter, Maria da Glória, then a child of seven years; but only after once more posing as a generous sovereign conferring liberal institutions on a grateful people by providing Portugal with a constitution or

[13] The first foreign government to recognize Brazil's independence was the United States, on May 26, 1824.

"Charter." Meanwhile his younger brother, Dom Miguel, was recognized as regent on condition of marrying his niece.[14]

Within four months of Dom Miguel's arrival in Lisbon in 1828, he was declared king by the absolutist party, and Maria da Glória was shipped off to England (the haven of most exiled princes from the Continent) and ultimately back to Brazil. Her father, nevertheless, continued to uphold her claims and gave her and her party in Portugal financial assistance. And so money and effort were expended on what Brazilians asserted was a private, dynastic quarrel. And when they learned that an expedition against Portugal had been outfitted and armed in England at the cost of Brazil, had sailed under the Brazilian flag, to outwit British neutrality laws, ostensibly for Brazil, and had been fired on by British warships to prevent its landing in the Azores, nationalistic opposition in Brazil rose to fever heat.

Anglo-Brazilian relations left something to be desired for other reasons. Great Britain in its world-wide endeavor to destroy the African slave trade, in a series of conventions beginning with the Commercial Treaty of 1810, had bound the government in Brazil to a progressive reduction of the traffic. By another treaty in 1826 Dom Pedro was constrained to promise total abolition three years after ratification.[15] As Brazilian prosperity was based on plantation agriculture and slave labor, and much capital was involved in the traffic, the repercussion in Brazilian public opinion may easily be imagined, especially as Parliament was customarily informed of international agreements only after the event.

[14] The Emperor's letter of renunciation, however, included the reservation that it would be of effect only if two conditions were met: the marriage of Maria da Glória and Dom Miguel, and the acceptance of the Charter by all the Portuguese. As neither condition was fulfilled, Dom Pedro would seem to have remained in theory, until his abdication in 1831, both King of Portugal and Emperor of Brazil. Alfredo Valladão, *Da Acclamação à maioridade, 1822–1840* (São Paulo, 1934), p. 314.

[15] See below, pp. 89–90.

An even more serious source of popular dissatisfaction was a war with Argentina over the possession of what now is the Republic of Uruguay. Behind it is a long story, the genesis of which extends back to the sixteenth century. Conflicting claims over the boundary between Spanish and Portuguese America in that area had left this marginal region a sort of no man's land, unoccupied until 1680 when Portuguese from Rio de Janeiro established a settlement, Colônia do Sacramento, on the eastern bank of the Río de la Plata directly opposite Buenos Aires. The Spaniards retorted some forty-five years later by founding the city of Montevideo. In every war in Europe in which Spain and Portugal were found in opposing camps, Colônia was seized by the Spaniards in Buenos Aires, and restored in the subsequent peace. The dispute persisted until 1777 when a treaty determining the boundary between Brazil and the Spanish Empire gave the Banda Oriental (Eastern Bank) definitely to Spain as part of the newly created Viceroyalty of the Río de la Plata.

When in 1810 and later the independence struggle developed in the Viceroyalty, patriots on the two sides of the river came to blows over the question that was to be a critical issue later in Brazil: unitary or centralized government versus federalism. And the Portuguese in Brazil under Dom João VI [16] seized the occasion to invade the area again and ultimately to annex it as the Cisplatine Province. This was in 1821, the year before Brazil's independence. But four years later, during Dom Pedro's reign, the Spanish population on the eastern shore revolted, drove out the quislings among them, and sought

---

[16] Earlier, in 1809–10, a confusing element in Portuguese relations with the Río de la Plata had been the intrigues of Carlota Joaquina, wife of Dom João and sister of Ferdinand VII of Spain, to obtain recognition by the Spanish colonists as regent in her brother's absence. Carlota Joaquina, hard featured, immoral, but superior in intelligence and courage to her husband, who both hated and feared her, was throughout her lifetime the real leader of the Portuguese absolutist party.

annexation to Argentina across the river. The result was a desultory and unpopular[17] war between Brazil and Argentina that lasted nearly three years and brought no great glory to either side. Eventually, through the mediation of Great Britain, whose commercial interests in the Río de la Plata were suffering, the contest ended in August 1828 in a compromise. This marginal area was to be neither Argentine nor Brazilian. It was set up as an independent republic, La Republica Oriental del Uruguay, a buffer state under the joint guarantee of its two neighbors.

The war's outcome ushered in an era in which the key to diplomacy on the Río de la Plata was the maintenance of an equilibrium by assuring the independence of the two little border republics, Uruguay and Paraguay. In the eyes of patriotic Brazilians, however, the conflict was a national disaster. A province had been lost, Brazilian arms defeated, the treasury drained by an inglorious war, and the prestige of the crown seriously impaired.

A humiliating episode was the mutiny of German and Irish mercenaries in the garrison of Rio de Janeiro in June 1828. Three years earlier a Major Schaeffer had been sent to Germany to recruit immigrants as colonists and soldiers, and a year later a Colonel Cotter went on a similar mission to Ireland. In all, several thousand officers and men were thus enlisted, many of them vagabonds, drunkards, or criminals, the off-scourings of Europe. Lured by false promises, in Rio they were miserably housed and fed, insubordinate, and subject to heavy corporal punishments, the most savage and cruel of the officers being often of their own nationality. In the second week of June, outraged by the infliction of 230 stripes on a German soldier who failed to salute an officer in civilian

[17] The Chamber of Deputies consistently refused requests by the government for funds to prosecute the war with greater vigor, and opposed recourse to foreign mercenaries.

clothes, the soldier's company mutinied against the commandant, and in searching for him in the city started a general
riot in which the Irish heartily joined. For several days the
city was at their mercy, with murders, robberies, destruction
of property, and horrible cruelties inflicted by the rioters and
by the populace, mostly Negroes, that opposed them; until
the offending barracks were stormed and the leaders imprisoned on ships in the harbor. Most of the Irish, some two
thousand, were shipped back to Ireland, and about four hundred were settled in Bahia. Many of the Germans were sent
to join the German colony of São Leopoldo in Rio Grande do
Sul.[18]

A source of popular solicitude was the disordered state of
public finances, in which was involved the Bank of Brazil, set
up as a bank of issue shortly after the royal flight to America.
When Dom João VI, his courtiers, and officials prepared to
return to Lisbon in 1821, virtually all the banknotes were in
their hands, and being suddenly presented for redemption almost ruined the bank. Under Dom Pedro I, who had no
understanding of budgetary matters and treated the imperial
treasury as his private purse, the perennial deficits of the government were met with increasing issues of paper money
whose value in foreign exchange sank proportionately. Gold
and silver were driven from circulation, leaving only a copper
coinage crudely minted and widely counterfeited, which became a financial headache in the following decade. When bad
management and popular dissatisfaction caused Parliament in
1829 to order the liquidation of the bank, it was found that
the notes in circulation almost exactly equaled the debt to the
bank of the national treasury. As the bank in spite of its shortcomings was virtually the only source of commercial credit
in the country, liquidation may not have been an unmixed

[18] J. Capistrano de Abreu, "Sob o primeiro império," in *Ensaios e estudos*,
2a série ([Rio de Janeiro], 1932), pp. 101–127.

blessing. The low state of public credit was reflected in a government loan of the same year, bearing 5 per cent interest and sold to foreign bankers at 52!

One more circumstance must be mentioned in reviewing the relations between Dom Pedro I and his subjects, the role of a Madame Pompadour. The wife of Dom Pedro was the archduchess Maria Leopoldina of Austria, faithful and intelligent, but homely,[19] careless in attire, and like her husband devoted to riding and hunting. Interested in literature and the natural sciences, and dedicated to the cause of Brazilian independence, she had been an early friend and admirer of José Bonifácio. In January 1821, when he with the delegation from São Paulo was traveling to Rio de Janeiro to fortify the resolution of Dom Pedro, she rode out to meet the group en route, was apparently the first to inform him of his appointment by her husband as Minister of State and Foreign Affairs, and urged him to accept. And during Dom Pedro's absence from Rio in August–September 1822, Leopoldina as acting regent presided over the Council of Ministers and with them urged upon Dom Pedro the decision echoed in the Cry of Ipiranga. It was on this same visit to São Paulo that the Prince met Domitila de Castro whom he later made Marquesa de Santos.

The concubine was by all accounts a fascinating young woman, twenty-four years of age, daughter of an army officer, already married and mother of several children. Although Dom Pedro was an unconscionable libertine, there is no doubt of his sincere and constant affection for Domitila. She bore him five children, three of whom died in infancy. The little palace he built for her just outside the gates of São Cristóvão survives today as one of the most charming examples of the Luso-Brazilian architecture of that period. Her influence with

[19] Described by a visiting foreigner as short and stout, with German features, reddish complexion, and without the grace and refinement of her sister, Marie Louise, the wife of Napoleon.

her imperial lover in the interest of friends and hangers-on, and the frankness with which he flaunted the liaison before the public, created a host of bitter enemies, and shocked, it is said, Brazilian public opinion generally not oversqueamish in such matters. On the other hand, much of the evil said of Domitila seems to be pure gossip.

The Empress, whose kindness and charities made her very popular with her subjects, asked the Austrian ambassador to inform her father that she was very unhappy. Her health failing, she died in December 1826, shortly after a violent quarrel with Dom Pedro over the Marquesa. Although Domitila maintained her ascendency, the Emperor became engrossed with the idea of a new marriage with a European princess, and in 1829 he discarded her as a condition of marrying the lovely Amelia of Leuchtenberg, granddaughter of Napoleon and Josephine de Beauharnais. The Marquesa retired to her native province where she spent most of her remaining life, married again, and on her death in 1867 received the homage of the best families of São Paulo.

One can scarcely agree with some historians who count the Marquesa de Santos as one of the reasons for the political crisis of 1831. It was the bitter memory of the conflict between the Emperor and the Constituent Assembly of 1823, the inability of Dom Pedro to govern within the bounds of his own constitution, and his invidious association with the unpopular Portuguese that poisoned the relations between sovereign and subjects throughout the reign. "Had there existed real bonds of sympathy and mutual good will between executive and legislature, some understanding might have been achieved." But everything seemed to conspire to divide the two powers. "What an allurement [for Dom Pedro] there was in the mere act of governing, of realizing great undertakings, of making wars, of creating anything freely within the half formless mass of the vast empire, and creating sovereignly according to the best divine technique, without the collaboration and the counsel of these demiurges who were deputies and senators . . . !" [20]

After the exile of the Andradas, the outstanding personality in Parliament came to be Bernardo de Vasconcelos, a deputy from Minas Gerais, a paralytic, but of immense energy and boundless eloquence. A liberal, "imbued with constitutionalism, the excellencies of the representative regime, the rights of man," he had also a saving sense of realities and of the concrete that marked him off from many of his doctrinaire contemporaries. Called the "master of parliamentarism in Brazil," it was he who in the first session in 1826 presented a bill obliging ministers and secretaries of state to submit annual reports of their administration and be present at budgetary hearings, a concession tacitly accepted by the government two years later. He was also the principal author of the Criminal Code of 1830, "the first code autonomous and characteristic of Latin America, serving as a basis for the Spanish Code of 1848, for Russia, and for Latin American legislation in general." [21]

Only twice did Dom Pedro try to govern with a ministry that reflected an accord with the lower, elected Chamber, and each time for a few months only. In November 1827 he called several deputies of a moderate, liberal persuasion into the cabinet, notably Pedro de Araújo Lima, destined to have a distinguished political career. Two of the exiled Andrada brothers, Antônio Carlos and Martim Francisco, were allowed to return to Brazil, followed later by José Bonifácio. Ministers appeared before the Chamber for interpellation, gave explanations freely and courteously, and submitted reports. But

[20] O. T. de Sousa, *Bernardo Pereira de Vasconcellos* (Rio de Janeiro, 1937), p. 60.
[21] *Ibid., passim.*

after the mutiny of the German and Irish mercenaries in the following June, the Emperor dismissed the Minister of War, and the liberals in solidarity with him resigned.

In December 1829, Dom Pedro was induced, perhaps by José Bonifácio back from exile and reconciled with him, to form a ministry under Felisberto Brant Pontes, Marquês de Barbacena, who had recently returned from Europe with the new empress, Dona Amelia, after an extremely difficult but highly successful diplomatic mission. All but one were titled men, but all were Brazilians. The new government made every effort to win over public opinion by a strictly constitutional conduct and was strongly supported by a newly elected Parliament. The Emperor was even prevailed upon, with great difficulty, to dismiss his hated "kitchen cabinet" of low-born and corrupt Portuguese cronies, two of whom were sent abroad as chargés d'affaires to Naples and Sweden. Parliament closed its sessions on November 30, 1830, after having successfully accomplished a budgetary law (for the first time), a law regulating the armed forces, and the Criminal Code. But in the meantime the skies had suddenly clouded, and events moved rapidly to a climax.

On September 14 news had arrived in Rio de Janeiro of the July Revolution in Paris and the dethronement of the King. In France there had been a political situation somewhat analogous to that in Brazil. Since the restoration of the Bourbon monarchy in 1816, France had lived under a constitution or Charter, which in fact was a model in part for the Brazilian Constitution of 1824. The King in the late 1820's, Charles X, like Dom Pedro made little effort to abide by its precepts. More, he plotted deliberately to subvert the Charter and restore an uninhibited royal absolutism. The outcome was a revolution in the streets of Paris in July 1830 that drove Charles X from the country. The revolution was really sparked by republicans and radicals, but moderate monarchists managed to seize control of events and succeeded in substituting the "July Monarchy" of the Duke of Orleans who became King as Louis Philippe. These developments were not lost on the minds of liberals in Brazil, nor for that matter, of liberals in the Netherlands, Poland, and Italy, for the year 1830, like 1820, was again a year of revolutions in Europe.

The effect of the news from France, says Armitage, an eyewitness, was "electric." Many individuals in Rio, São Paulo, Bahia and Pernambuco illuminated their houses. Only Dom Pedro apparently did not see the writing on the wall. Influenced by the intrigues and insinuations of his exiled Portuguese intimates, he gradually withdrew his support from Barbacena and finally dismissed him under humiliating circumstances. One by one the other members of the cabinet were replaced. In São Paulo public demonstrations over the events in Paris were violently repressed by the *ouvidor* or chief magistrate, and a protesting Italian journalist was barbarously assassinated. Journals throughout Brazil took up the hue and cry, the more extreme calling for abolition of the monarchy and substitution by a federal republic. In Minas Gerais, to which the Emperor and Empress made a visit early in 1831 to stem the widespread discontent, Dom Pedro was coolly received, and many of the honors and decorations he distributed were publicly rejected by their recipients. An imperial proclamation issued in Ouro Preto in February calling the opposition revolutionaries and self-seekers, only increased the popular excitement.

On Dom Pedro's return to Rio de Janeiro in March, his thoughts turned to abdication. His American mission ended, he would devote himself to the cause of his daughter, the exiled Queen of Portugal. His arrival in the capital was the signal for street encounters between Brazilian youths and celebrating Portuguese absolutists, culminating on March 13 in the *noite das garrafadas*, or "night of the beer bottles." In response to a vigorous protest presented by twenty-four liberal members of Parliament, the Emperor then appointed a new ministry composed entirely of Brazilians. But as public agitation continued, within three weeks he dismissed it for another consisting of unpopular aristocrats, the "ministry of the marquises." When the news was published on April 6, popular ferment spread throughout the city. Groups streamed through the streets, a crowd of several thousand gathered in the Campo de Sant'Ana, and toward evening a delegation of magistrates repaired to the palace to demand the restoration of the fallen ministry. Dom Pedro replied in the negative — it would be a denial of the imperial prerogative. He said that he would "do everything for the people, but nothing by the people." Announcement of the response clinched the Revolution, in which by midnight the garrison also joined. Deserted on all sides, even by the Emperor's Battalion at the palace, Dom Pedro, alone in his study, early next morning wrote out an Act of Abdication in favor of his son, also named Pedro, then in his fifth year, and with tears in his eyes handed it to an emissary of the rebels. He also requested that José Bonifácio, his old minister of the halcyon days of 1822, be appointed by Parliament as the boy's tutor.

Dom Pedro and his Empress immediately embarked on a British warship, the *Warspite*, and sailed for Europe, taking with them such gold and silver as existed in the liquidated Bank of Brazil. As the French chargé d'affaires wrote, the Emperor "knew better how to abdicate than to reign . . . on this unforgettable night the sovereign rose beyond himself, and revealed a presence of mind, a firmness and a dignity, that declared what this unhappy prince might have been, with a better education, and if more noble examples had come before his eyes." [22] In Portugal, as Duke of Braganza and knight errant, he undertook the reconquest of the throne usurped

[22] Quoted by Oliveira Lima in *O Império brasileiro, 1822–1889*, p. 22.

by his brother, Dom Miguel. This objective achieved against great odds, Dom Pedro as regent restored the crown to his daughter, Queen Maria II, and died in 1834.

Dom Pedro I, an ambitious, quixotic, impetuous young Portuguese prince who chose to throw in his lot with the Brazilians in their aspirations for political independence, was at the outset extremely popular. But during a reign of nine years he became increasingly estranged from the majority of his subjects because, although romantically imagining himself a liberal, he was congenitally an autocrat; because he was believed to put dynastic considerations above the true interests of his adopted Brazil; and because, himself a Portuguese, he chose to surround himself with reactionary ministers and courtiers of Portuguese birth to the practical exclusion of patriotic Brazilians. On the other hand, Brazilians remember that it was Dom Pedro's indispensable collaboration and initial liberal enthusiasms that made independence possible virtually without bloodshed, that preserved the country from dismemberment, and from the anarchy and militarism that afflicted its Spanish neighbors.

Chapter Three

* * * * * * * * * * * *

EXPERIMENTS WITH REPUBLICANISM

MINORITY OF DOM PEDRO II

The Revolution of April 1831 was a nativist revolt. The motive force was resentment against the Portuguese and their preponderance in the government. To this extent it was a reiteration of the Cry of Ipiranga of September 7, 1822. But the political ferment also had a republican and federalist source, and given the radical character of the movement the logical consequence might seem to be a republic. The abdication, however, came as something of a surprise to many of the more moderate and conservative opposition. The agitation had been carried much farther than they anticipated. Many were impelled to turn back, become more conservative, unite to take over the Revolution and preserve the monarchy; fearful also that with federalism in the air and provincialism run rampant, the precarious national unity might be destroyed.

So April 7 proved to be another Day of Dupes. The radicals, or *exaltados*, who projected and accomplished the revolt, found themselves displaced by moderates who were determined to maintain the political status quo, as had happened in France the year before. Conservative, even "Portuguese," influence was not immediately eliminated from the conduct of affairs.

The *exaltados*, on the other hand, in their exasperation were driven into an extreme federalist and even separatist agitation that threw the provinces into a condition of anarchy. As the distinguished statesman and historian, Joaquim Nabuco, later remarked, it was impossible to achieve a revolution without the radicals, and impossible to govern with them.

A notable role in the guidance of public opinion in these critical years was played by a journalist, Evaristo Ferreira da Veiga, the greatest of the early publicists of Brazil. A man of humble origin, he started out as a bookseller, but as proprietor and editor of a newspaper, *Aurora Fluminense*, became a writer of great elegance and fine irony, of discernment and independence, and set a style for later Brazilian journalism. His newspaper, established in 1827, was written with simplicity and dignity, without the affectations and bombast of the radical sheets, or the arrogance and servility of official newspapers. Evaristo exerted an immense influence on the course of events we have reviewed, always on the side of order and honest observance of the Constitution. He was a leader in the group of liberals who in March had protested to the Emperor against the insults and provocations of the Portuguese party, and in the disorders of the thirteenth and fourteenth his house had been stoned by the absolutists. In the crisis of April he ranged himself momentarily with the *exaltados* in their demand for federalization; and in the difficult days of the Regency he continued to play an important political role until his untimely death in 1836, exercising a kind of moral ascendency in the interest of moderation, of monarchy, and of liberal, constitutional integrity.

After the abdication a special session of Parliament, as provided in the Constitution, appointed a regency of three by which Brazil was governed for two years. It ushered in, however, a decade of extraordinary confusion, struggles between radicals and conservatives, between centralists and federalists, between Brazilians and Portuguese, between republicans and monarchists, between the north and south, popular tumults stirred up by radical demagogues. Most of the important cities were scenes of these commotions.

The army, demoralized by the far from exemplary part it had played in the April Revolution, got entirely out of hand, and there were repeated mutinies in the garrisons. The army had never been a force for order and legality in the young Empire. The Portuguese element in the beginning, and then the mercenaries called in because of the resistance of the population to military service in the war against Argentina, together with the heedlessness of Dom Pedro I in matters of generally recognized military practice and discipline, had hindered the growth of any regular and systematic organization. Arrogant and undisciplined, believing that everything could be settled by resort to arms, it became the ready tool of any popular agitator or demagogue, and often the source of riot and sedition. Even in the capital, soldiers mutinied more than once, and the infant Emperor had to be hastily carried from the palace to a place of greater safety. The Minister of Justice in the early days of the Regency, Diogo Antônio Feijó, resorted to the creation of a National Guard in Rio to quell uprisings in and about the capital.

The interregnum of the Regency was consequently a period of successive rebellions, military and popular, some essentially monarchical, others confessedly republican, in almost all the provinces of Brazil: in Pernambuco and Alagoas from 1831 to 1835, and in Ceará in 1832, inspired by reactionaries who wanted to recall Dom Pedro I; in Maranhão in 1831–32, followed later by a bloody civil war from 1838 to 1840; in Bahia in the years 1832 to 1835, coinciding with a servile Negro insurrection, and again in 1837–38; in Minas Gerais in 1833; and in Mato Grosso a brutal uprising against foreigners in 1834. The most extended and violent upheavals, however, occurred in the two peripheral provinces of Pará in the north and Rio Grande do Sul, both extreme manifestations of a nativism and federalism that was soon transmuted into secession.

The so-called *Cabanagem* of Pará, originating in a long-standing feud between the nativists or *filantrópicos* and the *caramurús* or Portuguese faction, degenerated into a barbarous civil war in which legal governors were deposed or assassinated by insurgent armies of Indians and half-castes, and the province desolated by pillage, famine, and disease. Beginning in January 1835, it was supposedly suppressed in May of the following year, but hostilities on the margins of a tropical Amazonian wilderness continued until finally extinguished in March of 1840.[1]

More serious was a republican and separatist revolt in the extreme south, in Rio Grande do Sul, the *Revolução Farroupilha* (Revolution of the Ragamuffins). It began with the seizure of the capital, Pôrto Alegre, in September 1835 and lasted for ten years. Starting as a conflict between "ins" and "outs," it soon developed into a war for independence. Its causes were a compound of extreme regionalism, protest against "discriminatory" taxation and unsympathetic governors imposed by the central government, but more immediately the intense bitterness between the liberal and reactionary parties.

Rio Grande do Sul has always played an exceptional role in Brazilian history. It lies next door to Uruguay and Argentina and is physiographically merely an extension of the former, with no natural boundary between the two areas. It was eminently a pastoral society of cattle barons and landless, roaming *gaúchos*. Brazilians and Uruguayans lived, and had cattle ranches, on both sides of the frontier. The *gaúcho*, as a social and cultural type, was common to both areas, and contraband

[1] Basílio Magalhães, *Estudos de história do Brasil* (São Paulo, 1940), pp. 211–243.

trade and cattle rustling were endemic. The Riograndenses were always mixed up in the political quarrels of Uruguay from the days of its independence, and they always felt rather remote from Rio de Janeiro and its politicians. Insurgents on either side could easily find asylum among friends and relatives across the border, or obtain arms and supplies from the same quarter.

Given the political circumstances both within Brazil and on the Río de la Plata, extraneous influences inevitably injected themselves into the rebellion. Malcontent individuals from unruly provinces farther north were involved. Political exiles from Italy, notably Guiseppe Garibaldi and Luigi Rossetti, gave yeoman service in this so-called Republic of Piratim, the former as a sailor and soldier, the latter as an intellectual leader and mentor of the movement. The Uruguayan caudillo, Fructuoso Rivera, from 1838 was in open alliance with the Riograndenses, and sent them arms, horses, and money. He without question harbored the vaster ambition of uniting Rio Grande and Uruguay in a large buffer state that would include also the Argentine "mediterranean" provinces of Entre Ríos and Corrientes. And so akin on the two sides of the border were the social and political mores of a rude, pastoral society that such an eventuality did not seem unrealistic.

Within a year of the outbreak, imperial forces had recovered Pôrto Alegre and most of the seaboard towns, and in October 1836 they defeated and captured the able and popular leader, Bento Gonçalves da Silva. Meantime, as appeals to the Regency for a settlement had been ignored, the insurgents proclaimed Rio Grande an independent republic. In the interior the imperialists were unable to make serious headway, and the escape and return of Bento Gonçalves in 1837 gave new impetus to the revolt. An expedition from Rio Grande in 1839 set up a republic in the neighboring province of Santa

Catarina, but it survived only four months. Although the nascent republic suffered from lack of resources, internal rivalries, and military reverses, the struggle dragged on, owing largely to the incompetence or divided authority of the officials sent from Rio de Janeiro; until the arrival late in 1842 of a brilliant army officer, Luiz Alves de Lima e Silva, Barão and later Conde and Duque de Caxias, Brazil's most famous military figure. Fresh from the suppression of uprisings in Maranhão, Minas Gerais, and São Paulo, and combining martial pressures with political address and forbearance, he was able early in 1845 to impose an honorable peace and submission. Whether the republican leaders ever seriously contemplated complete separation from the Empire has been a matter of debate ever since. Barão de Caxias became Conde de Caxias, was promoted to the rank of field marshal, and shortly after was chosen life senator from Rio Grande do Sul.

Amid all the commotions of the decade of the Regency, the most stable area, the "ballast" of the Empire, was in the south-central provinces, Rio de Janeiro, São Paulo, and Minas Gerais, provinces that had assumed the lead in the secession from Portugal and that have continued to exert a political preponderance as states in the Federal Republic down to our own day. But in the national Parliament and in the public press party strife ran riot. In the government the most commanding figure was a somewhat radical priest from São Paulo, Diogo Antônio Feijó, Minister of Justice. Feijó was one of the most eminent personages of his generation. An esteemed patriot, and a man of unquestioned integrity and disinterestedness, he was an ardent defender of order and legality. With Vasconcelos and Evaristo da Veiga he led the forces working for moderation and equilibrium against the excesses of revolutionary radicalism. As minister he displayed great energy and decision, but he was also inclined to be dogmatic, impatient of opposition, and he made many enemies. As stated above, the suppression of violence and sedition in Rio in 1831–32 was chiefly his accomplishment.

In the early days of the Regency, political parties began to assume a definite profile. Under the personal rule of the first Emperor there were liberals (many of them hoping for a republic), moderate monarchists, and royalist reactionaries, but they did not group themselves into more or less disciplined parties. Sympathies and antipathies revolved around the person of the Emperor, and the nationalist issue, Brazilian versus Portuguese, animated people more than political ideologies. After the abdication, party lines became more clearly defined: monarchist liberals led by Vasconcelos and Evaristo; extreme liberals, the *exaltados*, many of them cryptic republicans; and the *caramurús* or *restauradores*, whose material interests in many cases had been bound up with the former regime and who schemed for a restoration of Dom Pedro I.[2] Reflecting these trends was a host of journals in Rio that descended to the extremity of indecency, insult, and invective. With the open intrigues of the *restauradores* was associated, rightly or wrongly, the name of José Bonifácio, tutor of the young Emperor. Feijó demanded his dismissal, and so great was the agitation in Parliament that members of the government, including the Regents, projected a parliamentary *coup d'état:* conversion of the Chamber of Deputies into a national constituent assembly without the collaboration of the Senate, stronghold of the reactionaries. Wiser counsels prevailed and the Chamber failed to act. Yet in March 1833 the *caramurús* staged a military revolt in Minas Gerais that seized the capital, Ouro Preto, and held it for several months.

Constitutional reform, however, was urgent, to satisfy the

[2] The *restauradores* were banded together in a *Sociedade Militar*, the moderates in a *Sociedade Defensora da Liberdade e da Independência*, the radicals in the *Sociedade Federal*.

liberal imperatives of the Revolution; and as early as October 1831 the Chamber had approved a project much more radical than the measures finally embodied in the Additional Act of August 1834. This latter series of constitutional amendments, of which Vasconcelos was the principal author, was a partial concession to the regional and democratic forces then at large. The provinces were given autonomous, elected legislative assemblies with extended political powers. Entailing of estates, one of the mainstays of aristocracy in an agrarian society, was abolished. And the Council of State, under the Constitution an advisory body of the sovereign and regarded in the time of Dom Pedro I as a bulwark of reaction, was suppressed. This was not federation, for provincial governors or presidents were still appointed by the central power, which also retained a partial veto over local legislation. The revolutionary excesses in many of the provinces, including Rio de Janeiro and Minas Gerais, and the political inexperience and low cultural level of most of the population would have made genuine federalism a serious threat to national unity.

One of the innovations in the reforms of 1834, in order to strengthen the executive power, was the substitution of a single regent for a board of three, and in the following year Diogo Antônio Feijó was so chosen by Parliament. He was Regent for two years, in many ways an ill-starred interval. His election coincided almost exactly with the outbreak of revolt in Rio Grande do Sul. A week before installation he suffered a first attack of paralysis, and although he continued to reveal his old courage and energy, it was in a mood of pessimism and distrust. He faced rebellion in Rio Grande and Pará and instituted vigorous military measures against both. Temperamentally an authoritarian, he refused to be the rubber stamp of legislative policy, ignored or defied the parliamentary majority, and chose at will ministers who merely echoed his own ideas. And the leader of the opposition was his former

political ally, the astute and indefatigable Vasconcelos.[3] The
breach between the Chamber and the Regent became every
day more critical, the attacks of the opposition more caustic
and envenomed, until Feijó, incapable of adaptation or compromise, unable to make headway against the rebellion in Rio
Grande do Sul, wearily gave up the struggle. In September
1837 he resigned in favor of Pedro de Araújo Lima, who for
several years had been president of the Chamber of Deputies.
Of a disposition very different from that of Feijó, courteous,
tolerant, dispassionate, he became the leader of what was to
emerge as the Conservative Party of the Second Empire, a
coalition of the constitutionalists of 1831 and the *restauradores,* who with the death of the first Emperor in Europe in
September 1834 had been left without a rallying cry. Later,
as Marquês de Olinda, Araújo Lima was to be one of the bul-
warks of the monarchy.

The cabinet that he immediately selected, with Vasconcelos
in the key role as Minister of Government and of Justice, was
a ministry of talents drawn from the parliamentary majority.
It also reflected a growing desire in all classes for some measure of relief from the incessant political turmoil, for a return
to order and tranquillity. And in the van of this conservative
alignment was the coffee aristocracy of the province of Rio
de Janeiro, the great agricultural proprietors of the celebrated
Paraíba Valley, who were to provide the orientation to Bra-

[3] The charge sometimes made that Feijó, himself a priest, aimed at setting
up a schismatic Brazilian Church separated from Rome, is apparently a
libel. It presumably grew out of extreme statements made by both sides of
a bitter controversy between Vasconcelos and the Regent over the latter's
management of negotiations with the Papacy regarding the confirmation of
the Brazilian candidate for the bishopric of Rio de Janeiro. Involved was
also the desire of Feijó to invite from Europe Moravian missionaries to work
among the Indians. He had earlier advocated the abolition of clerical celibacy
by act of Parliament, with or without the concurrence of the Papacy.
Alfredo Ellis Junior, *Feijó e a primeira metade do século XIX* (São Paulo,
1940), pp. 149–173, 415–433; Vitor de Azevedo, *Feijó* (São Paulo, 1942), pp.
132–136. Cf. below, p. 114.

zilian politics during the next generation. But the new government was no more successful than its predecessor in restoring peace in the south or maintaining it in the north. As the Regency seemed unable to check the tendency to national disintegration, the stratagem was conceived of restoring the prestige of the central authority by calling on the young Emperor to rule, assisted by an advisory council. The idea was first broached early in 1837, when the Prince was only twelve years old, and sentiment steadily gained ground for anticipating Dom Pedro's majority. Again, as in 1822, the throne was to be the "providential instrument" for saving the unity of the nation. And the proposal received its most enthusiastic support from the Liberals, who hoped thereby to consolidate their influence with the sovereign.

With the opening of the Parliament's sessions in 1840 the project made rapid headway. In April was formed a Society for the Promotion of the Majority under the presidency of Antônio Carlos de Andrada. The society approached Dom Pedro secretly through members of his entourage, and were assured of his compliance. "I wish it and am very glad that this undertaking be achieved by the Andradas and their friends," was the reply apparently received. Confident of the connivance of the young Prince, the *maioristas* redoubled their efforts. Declarations were introduced into both Chambers, popular agitation was whipped up outside, and for several months there was violent debate and great confusion in the Parliament, while noisy crowds filled the galleries. The Conservatives would have preferred proceeding by constitutional amendment, and first buttressing the government by revival of the Council of State and reforms in the criminal code and administration of the exchequer. But since it was impossible to stem the current, the Regent decided to try at least to divert it for several months until December 2, Dom Pedro's fifteenth birthday. Possibly thereby the Liberals would be deprived of some of the advantage of their initiative. On July 22, suddenly recalling the redoubtable Bernardo de Vasconcelos to head the ministry, Araújo Lima issued a decree proroguing Parliament. Recovering from their original shock, the *maiorista* deputies, followed by a crowd, repaired to the Senate building, where with the senators they held a noisy rump session and voted to send a mixed delegation to appeal to the Emperor to save the nation and the throne by taking over at once the reins of government. Consummating the semi-comedy, Dom Pedro after due consideration, and in the presence of the Regent, who had also arrived at the palace, signified his willingness to do so. The following morning the two chambers met in a general assembly and formally invested him with the imperial authority. In the afternoon Dom Pedro took the oath of office, and this was followed by three days of public celebrations — illuminations, fireworks, and Te Deums in the churches. Dom Pedro II was ceremoniously crowned a year later, in July 1841.

All that had happened was unconstitutional, nothing more or less than a parliamentary *coup d'état*. The Constitution required that the heir remain a minor until he was eighteen years of age. Dom Pedro was scarcely fifteen. But there is no doubt that public sentiment, wearied of uncertainty and disorder, was strongly behind it. The conspirators, too, quickly received their reward. The two Andrada brothers, Antônio Carlos and Martim Francisco, and three other leaders of the *maiorista* group were accorded portfolios in a newly organized and rather heterogeneous ministry. Given the personal prestige of Antônio Carlos and his position as leader of the *maioridade*, with parliamentary and popular support behind him, the decision was inevitable.

Joaquim Nabuco observed in his celebrated book, *Um Estadista do Império*, that the Regency was in fact a republic, a "provisional republic" which was granted the opportunity to demonstrate that the institution of monarchy was unnecessary if not an anachronism. From this angle its failure was complete. The nine years of the interregnum had witnessed a succession of political shocks that threatened to rend the national fabric, subversive regionalistic or republican movements in nearly every province of the Empire. Brazil seemed on the point of breaking up, as had the Spanish Empire, into a congeries of quarrelsome independent states. The extreme liberalism engendered by the Revolution of 1831 was tried and found wanting. In 1840 public ratification of the Emperor's majority was motivated by the instinct of self-preservation. The prestige of monarchy became the symbol of peace and a guarantee of the survival of Brazilian nationality.

As Nabuco also observed, what made the great reputation of statesmen of that era was not what they accomplished in the way of reform, but the resistance they opposed to anarchy. Nevertheless, this experiment with "republicanism" had not been entirely sterile. It had accomplished something in the way of legal codification, improvement of administrative practice, creation of a Public Archive and a School of Agriculture. The famous Colégio Dom Pedro II was founded by government decree in 1837 and became the peculiar concern of Vasconcelos. The Regency upheld the liberty of the press at a time when liberty was interpreted as unbridled license, and greatly stimulated the emergence of a genuine public opinion. In the economic sphere it took the first steps to promote the construction of railways, and steam navigation between Rio de Janeiro and the northern ports. The fiscal administration was reorganized on a basis that prevailed to the end of the Empire, and the tax structure improved over the chaotic and unscientific practices inherited from colonial times. Deficits in the national treasury, it is true, were chronic, but progress was made in ridding the country of an exclusively copper coinage and the notes of the defunct Bank of Brazil.

Dom Pedro II, unlike his father, was born and educated in Brazil. To all intents and purposes an orphan since his father's withdrawal to Europe (although the latter kept in close touch by letter with his children), he had been brought up by tutors. His governess had been an elderly, cultured Portuguese lady, Mariana Carlota de Magalhães Coutinho. His tutor, after the dismissal of José Bonifácio for political reasons in December 1833, was an old aristocrat, Marquês de Itanhaen, of no great intellectual gifts, rather austere, very religious, but with a deep sense of duty. Under him served a Carmelite friar, Pedro de Santa Mariana, later titular Bishop of Crisopolis, and numerous instructors for special subjects. And they did an excellent job, determined to turn out a perfect sovereign. But it must have been a lonely childhood for the Prince, isolated from the healthy emulations and thrills of contact with other youth and strictly nurtured on the writers and precepts of the eighteenth-century Enlightenment.

Dom Pedro II proved to possess unusual personal qualities, in which he resembled his mother: high intelligence, with a prodigious memory and keen reasoning powers. And he was given an intellectual culture far beyond that of most of his Brazilian contemporaries. He ruled for forty-nine years, and developed a character in which honesty, urbanity, tolerance, and public spirit were united with political discretion. As Emperor he was very dignified but without ostentation, and in contrast to his Braganza father a model of the domestic virtues; catholic in his interests, well informed, a scholar as much as a ruler. Someone has said that if he had not been Emperor he would have been a school-teacher. He became a shrewd, placid, somewhat eccentric, royal philosopher, patron of science and literature. Victor Hugo called him "a grandson of Marcus Aurelius."

Dom Pedro guessed that monarchy would not long survive in Brazil. It was counter to the spirit of the times, at any rate in the Americas. So he tried to keep the nation satisfied by a policy of moderate conciliation. He once called himself the best republican in Brazil. He certainly was a much better republican than most of the presidential dictators ruling in the so-called democracies of Spanish America, then and now. "He used his great influence to guide the nation and its representatives toward solutions which he felt were most adequate for the common good." [4] Dom Pedro had his critics, of course, and criticism greatly increased toward the end of the reign. He was accused of resorting to personal influence in politics. He did so, as was required by the Moderating Power invested in him by the Constitution. Indeed it was inevitable in the political system that evolved under the Empire. But he failed toward the end, with all his conciliatory aims, to show sufficient initiative in meeting the demands for political reform, constitutional change, especially in the direction of decentralization, of greater local autonomy.

The first ministry of Dom Pedro II (the first of thirty-six ministries during his long reign) consisted mostly of Liberals, the parliamentary minority, headed by Antônio Carlos de Andrada, the eloquent but impassioned and often unscrupulous brother of José Bonifácio, who had led in the turbulence of the Constitutional Assembly of 1823 and in the intrigues and agitations of the *maioristas* in 1840. The Liberals in power immediately indulged in a wholesale dismissal of provincial presidents, judges, and other key officials, and their partisan and corrupt management of the ensuing general election caused a wave of popular protest. Dissensions within the ministry itself led to its resignation after eight months, and enabled Dom Pedro to call the Conservative majority into the government.

[4] Calógeras, *Formação histórica*, p. 335.

The new ministry, consisting of the cream of the Conservative leadership, made a complete *volte face*. To provide the government with the means of combating the anarchy induced by the exaggerated liberalism of the 1830's, it reversed some of the constitutional changes achieved by the Additional Act of 1834. The Council of State, a kind of directorate of elder statesmen, advisers of the Emperor appointed for life, which had been abolished in 1834, was restored. Radical excesses were checked by depriving the provincial legislatures of many of their powers. And administrative and judicial reforms were introduced that greatly strengthened the hand of the central executive. Under the Regency, judicial and police powers had been combined in the locally elected judges. By the law of December 3, 1841, the situation was reversed, judicial functions being entrusted to police authorities acting for the central government, a harsh and callous device that "for forty years maintained the solidity of the Empire." Moreover, as the Liberals expected to regain power when the new Chamber chosen under its auspices assembled, the Conservative ministry, with abundant evidence of corruption in the elections, induced the Emperor to dissolve it before meeting.

The immediate reaction of the Liberals was a revolt in 1842 in the two key provinces of Minas Gerais and São Paulo, easily defeated by the Barão de Caxias, who was then sent to Rio Grande do Sul, as stated above, to suppress the secessionist movement there. It is, however, interesting to note that the same Liberal Party, when it returned to power during the years 1844 to 1848, made no effort to revoke the Law of December 3, but rather made excellent use of it.

The last armed revolt of the reign (before 1889) was an insurrection in Pernambuco, classic land of revolution, in 1847–48. Behind it was a complex of all the ills that had beset the country since independence: violent anti-Portuguese prejudices that expanded into a xenophobia against all foreigners;

extreme factional rancors; personal rivalries and corrupt and riotous elections; hatred of the rural aristocracy by the radical urban populace of Recife, the provincial capital. The movement collapsed with the capture of Recife by the imperial forces, but without severe reprisals, for Dom Pedro imposed a policy of peace and magnanimity. It gave the Liberals, however, a prolonged setback, and the Conservatives a corresponding ascendency.

By 1850 Brazil was, so to speak, out of the woods, and the nation entered upon a career of peace and progress that was in sharp contrast to what was happening in most of the rest of the continent. It enjoyed one of the few enlightened governments south of the United States. It was not a democracy, for democracy was not possible in a nation that was mostly illiterate, and whose economy was based on slavery and the latifundium. The legislative power was enjoyed almost solely by the landed proprietors and their associates, the professional men, who formed the dominant social class. But the press was free, conscience was free, and individual liberties were fully guaranteed.

The Conservatives remained in control until 1844, when a new cabinet gave an orientation frankly Liberal to the administration that continued with many ministerial changes until 1848. Discord in Liberal ranks, reflecting in part the influence of revolutionary ferment in Europe, then ushered in a period of Conservative stewardship lasting until the early 1860's. Although the return of the Conservatives occasioned the revolt in Pernambuco already referred to, the new regime was to be one of the most notable in the history of the Empire.

From the beginning the Emperor, with all his youthful inexperience, frankly accepted a parliamentary procedure to the extent that the imperial ministry reflected the views of the majority in the national legislature. He took over the helm at a time when Brazilian society was rapidly being Europeanized, when foreign manners and styles in dress and cuisine were the mode. The same spirit of imitation prevailed in politics; the parliamentary practices of England and France were attentively followed so far as circumstances permitted. But circumstances in Brazil were not the same. For one thing, the Constitution of 1824, although it declared the imperial ministers responsible for their acts to Parliament, did not actually envisage a parliamentary system. The ministers were the personal choice of the sovereign, who appointed and dismissed them at pleasure. And the two houses of Parliament, the lower, elected Chamber of Deputies and the upper Chamber of Senators appointed for life, were of equal weight and authority. The Constitution did not give political supremacy to the elected chamber.

A parliamentary system also presupposed free elections and a widespread, intelligent electorate, so that Parliament really represented public opinion. In the event of conflict between Parliament and the ministers, the question could be referred back to the people in a general election. But in Brazil there was no widespread, intelligent electorate. Elections were therefore as a rule completely controlled by the local authorities, who in turn were directly or indirectly chosen by and responsible to the central government, or rather, to the party in power in the government. And elections, after the evil example set by the Liberals in 1840, were generally marked by gross fraud, violence, or persecution, especially under the police law of December 3, 1841. Elections always returned a government majority. That could mean a monopoly of power by one party or faction, as generally happened in the Spanish republics. If there was to be any alternation of parties, some outside influence had to intervene. In most of the Latin republics, the only resort was violence — revolution — to dislodge by force the party or faction that controlled the electoral process. It became, in fact, an accepted extra-constitutional way of changing the government.

In Brazil, fortunately, this change was accomplished by the personal intervention of a generally wise and conscientious Emperor under the Moderating Power, a function that placed on him a tremendous responsibility. The impatience and irritability of the opposition were restrained by the hope of an early recovery of control. If the Emperor was convinced that the cabinet no longer reflected the state of public opinion, or the best interests of the nation, he might dismiss it and call in another. If the new ministers did not command a sufficient following in Parliament, they could ask the Emperor for a general election, and by their control of the local electoral machinery see to it that a new Chamber was chosen that conformed to their wishes.

The English parliamentary system also implied that the sovereign (or the President of the Republic in France or Italy today) is independent of party politics. In Brazil under the Constitution of 1824 this immunity was extremely difficult to achieve, because the Emperor chose all the ministers. And in the 1840's there was a growing irritation in many political quarters over what was believed to be the "palace clique," individuals in the confidence of the young Emperor whose advice he was inclined to follow, and whose personal predilections were held responsible for the rapidly changing ministries in the years immediately following his Majority.[5]

[5] They were supposed to be chiefly Aureliano Coutinho, later Visconde de Sepetiba, and the majordomo of the palace, Paulo Barbosa da Silva, as well as those who had been closest to Dom Pedro as tutors and preceptors. Aureliano Coutinho, who had a distinguished record as cabinet minister and in various other administrative capacities both during the Regency and later, was believed to be the chief culprit and became the object of venomous calumnies. As a matter of fact Dom Pedro, although he admittedly liked Coutinho, from the beginning revealed that he had a mind of his own, and there seems to be little evidence that such a "clique" existed. See Helio Vianna, *Estudos de história imperial* (São Paulo, 1950), pp. 31–148.

Although we have no proof that there ever was such a clique, in July 1847 the Liberal ministry of that year, to assure greater political independence to the young Emperor, issued a decree creating the office of President of the Council of Ministers. The President of the Council became, in short, the Prime Minister who in consultation with the sovereign chose the other ministers, his colleagues in the cabinet. It was the coping to the Brazilian parliamentary procedure. It served to give greater unity to the cabinets, greater responsibility to the parties and their leaders, greater stability and coherence in the governmental process, and enabled the system to function with fair regularity. In spite of the shortcomings of parliamentarism in Brazil, the two major parties assumed form and substance, and a certain degree of party discipline. Alternating in regular succession, they learned when in the majority to respect the rights of the minority, and as a minority more or less gracefully to accept defeat. It was the great achievement of the statesmen of the first reign and the Regency, consummated under the second Emperor.

Chapter Four

THE EMPIRE COMES OF AGE

The decade of the 1850's is commonly recognized as the most notable in the history of the Brazilian Empire. The passions and discords of the Regency had burned themselves out. The principle of monarchy was for the time being accepted as the only assurance of national unity and survival. Brazil entered upon an era of unprecedented (for Latin America) tranquillity and economic development. The Conservative government that came into power in 1848 had brought into conjunction a group of men of marked political discernment and administrative competence. It reached its apogee in the organization under the Marquês de Paraná of the so-called Ministry of the Conciliation in 1853, in which appeared leaders of both parties, Conservative and Liberal, united in a common effort to erase past resentments and effect a program of administrative reorganization and material and intellectual progress.

Laws and decrees were promulgated on a great variety of subjects: public lands, taxation, public health, organization of the diplomatic service, etc. In 1849 were formulated the first rules for incorporated commercial companies, completed a decade later; and in 1850 a Commercial Code was issued that has remained substantially in force to the present. Caxias as Minister of War introduced needed reforms in the army. These multiform activities reflected a growing political maturity in public men and in the young Emperor himself — the coming of age of the Brazilian nation.

In education the Faculties of Medicine and Jurisprudence were reorganized, and primary and secondary programs reformed. "Letters tore off their classic colonial tatters; there was talk of a national opera, a national theater, João Caetano figuring as a new Moses; three epic poems were in course of elaboration, tragedies were being written; in the scientific commission of the North, not a single foreigner was admitted, because Brazilians were sufficient and would do a better work than the poor Martius and Saint Hilaire; the Instituto Histórico confronted without abashment the Institute of France. . . ." [1]

Economic progress under the circumstances was to be expected, for Dom Pedro ruled over a vast unexploited area rich in natural resources, and enjoying a settled government, at a time when the export of capital from Europe overseas was becoming an increasingly spectacular feature of world economy. Foreign capital was building the railways and industries of the United States; it did so on a smaller scale in Brazil and elsewhere in South America. And economic expansion plus political stability also spelled an increased impact of Brazil upon the economy and politics of its neighbors.

The great technological developments in transportation and industry in nineteenth-century Europe were, however, slower in reaching Latin America than the United States; and in Brazil they had been retarded in part by foreign competition embodied in tariff concessions to British trade ever since the flight of the Portuguese monarchy to America under British protection in 1808. Meantime relations with Great Britain had become increasingly difficult because of Britain's determined efforts to destroy the African slave trade, so strained that when the commercial treaty lapsed in 1844 the Bra-

[1] Capistrano de Abreu, "O Duque de Caxias," in *Ensaios e Estudos*, 2a série ([Rio de Janeiro], 1932), pp. 32–33.

zilian government refused to renew it.[2] In the same year Brazil essayed her first venture in protectionism, approximately doubling the duties on imports. It is therefore no mere coincidence that the first Brazilian manufactures started a few years later, in 1847 — the manufacture of textiles, which remained throughout the nineteenth century the nation's chief industrial activity. Moreover, with the consolidation of domestic peace after 1850, the Brazilian government finally took effective measures to eliminate the slave trade, a task to which it had been pledged for twenty-five years. And thereafter the considerable capital engaged in the traffic was diverted into railways and industrial enterprise.

Brazil began to adjust itself to the technological progress of the Western world. In 1851 was founded the second Bank of Brazil, two years later granted a monopoly of bank-note issue; and in 1853 was created a Rural Mortgage Bank which was to pay rich dividends. Over a score of banks appeared throughout the Empire in that decade, many of them short-lived. In 1854 the first railway line was opened to traffic, built with Brazilian resources — fifteen kilometers from Rio Bay to the foot of the mountains toward Petrópolis, the summer capital, and later climbing the *serra* to Petrópolis itself. In the same year illuminating gas was introduced on the streets of Rio. A company for the construction of a second railway to unite Rio with the interior of São Paulo and Minas Gerais was launched in 1855, today the Central of Brazil; and before the end of the decade railway lines were pushing inland from Salvador, Recife, and Santos, sponsored mostly by British, but also by some native, capital.[3] Steamship lines served the

[2] Commercial treaties with several other countries had been negotiated in the later years of the reign of Dom Pedro I granting most-favored-nation privileges, but all had expired by the early 1840's.

[3] With interest or dividends guaranteed by the imperial government. Most of the railway expansion came after the Paraguayan War. By the end of the reign nearly 6000 miles were in operation, and another thousand were under construction.

coastal cities from Pará to Rio Grande do Sul, and extended up to the Paraná and Paraguay Rivers to the inland province of Mato Grosso. An extraordinary record for these few years!

Progress might have been more rapid except for the tacit opposition — or at least the traditionalism, inertia, and indifference — of the politically dominant rural aristocracy. Even the establishment of an imperial institute of agriculture, long advocated by Dom Pedro, for many years met with no adequate response. The social and political preponderance of the landed proprietors (*fazendeiros*) was an inheritance from colonial times, when the entire life of the colony was concentrated on the great self-sustaining rural properties. In contrast to the situation in the Spanish colonies, the cities and towns of Brazil were to all intents and purposes dependencies of the country, occupied by minor officials, artisans, and merchants. Municipal government was dominated by the rural magnates who lived on their estates and occupied the town house only on special occasions of a religious festival or other solemnity. African slaves provided the labor, and monoculture was the rule, principally sugar in the early centuries, in the nineteenth century coffee. After independence, with the rise in importance of urban centers and the emergence of other occupations, political, bureaucratic, and professional, the rural *senhores* began to lose some of their privileged position. Nevertheless, under the Empire it was still the *fazendeiros* and their sons educated in the liberal professions who "monopolized politics, electing themselves or their candidates, dominating the parliaments, the ministries, in general all positions of authority, and effecting the stability of institutions by their unquestioned dominion. So unquestioned in reality that many representatives of this lordly class (*dos antigos senhores*) could with frequency give themselves the luxury of antitraditionalist inclinations, and even embark on some of the most important liberal movements . . . in our history." [4]

Most of the titled men were large landowners, for apart from agriculture, economic interests were identified chiefly with foreigners. The Brazilian nobility was also a new nobility, not based on claims of birth and descent as in the countries of old Europe. Before the nineteenth century titles were almost unknown in Brazil, although pretensions to aristocracy were as old as the colony, based on the possession of vast latifundia cultivated by great numbers of slaves. The concept of nobility was social and economic rather than racial. Some of the most eminent families had a distant aboriginal or African strain, usually dating from early colonial times. Titles of nobility were not hereditary, and entails were few.

The crown in Brazil was very prodigal in the bestowal of titles. This generosity began with Dom João VI and was continued by the first Emperor. The principal collaborators in the independence movement were so honored — barons, viscounts, marquises — and many others whose claim to distinction was less evident. Pedro Calmon tells us that Dom Pedro II established certain norms in conferring titles.[5] Members of the Council of State, generally men who had grown old in imperial service, were made marquises; presidents of the Supreme Court of Justice viscounts; commanders of the National Guard, who were almost invariably local territorial magnates, became barons — although the rule certainly was far from invariable. Dukedoms were reserved for princes of the blood, with one notable exception. The Marquês de Caxias, returning victorious from the Paraguayan War, was honored with the title of Duque. The lists did include a few

[4] Sérgio Buarque de Holanda, *Raízes do Brasil* (2nd ed., Rio de Janeiro, 1948), pp. 89–90.
[5] Pedro Calmon, *História social do Brasil* (São Paulo, 1937), pp. 290–293.

successful merchants and bankers, and occasionally some of the more notable military and naval officers, professors, and men of letters. And as in England there were always a few in public life who refused a title, preferring to remain known by their Christian and family names.

The traditional source of Brazil's wealth was sugar, the production of which was concentrated in the seaboard provinces of the northeast from Bahia to Paraíba. In the seventeenth century when Brazil was the chief supplier of sugar to Europe, it was there that colonial society assumed its characteristic patriarchal physiognomy. The competition of the West Indies in the eighteenth century and the spectacular exploitation of gold and diamonds in Minas Gerais, undermined sugar's preëminence in world markets; and the increasing cultivation of beet sugar in Europe in the nineteenth century intensified the crisis in Brazil's production of cane. Nevertheless sugar remained a not unimportant source of national wealth, and the planter aristocracy of Bahia and Pernambuco set the tone of Brazilian society and dominated parliamentary life in the early years of the second reign.

It was coffee, however, that became the economic mainstay of the "Second Empire," the principal source of national wealth; and it has continued to be so under the Republic. It is generally believed that coffee was brought from Cayenne (French Guiana) in 1723 to the province of Pará where it was cultivated and in small quantities exported to Europe. About 1770 it was carried to Rio de Janeiro, whence it spread into southern Minas Gerais and into the Paraíba Valley, the great natural highway reaching westward from Rio to the province of São Paulo. After 1850 the production of coffee increased by leaps and bounds, so that its export in the following decade first gave a favorable turn to Brazil's balance of trade. And in the later decades of Dom Pedro's long reign, it was more and more men drawn from the ranks of the Paraíba coffee magnates, or their *bacharel* sons and nephews, who served the Empire and crystallized the urgent political and economic issues of that era.

In the material expansion of the fifties, commercial and industrial corporations rapidly increased in number, bringing with them many monopolistic abuses due partly to the primitive state of corporation law. And overexpansion of credit, and extravagant and unbalanced national budgets, as normally happens, brought on economic and financial crises in 1858 and again in 1864. The key figure in these years was a Brazilian merchant-banker, statesman, and diplomat, Irineu Evangelista de Sousa, who became Barão and later Visconde de Mauá. A man of very modest antecedents, born in Rio Grande do Sul on the borders of Uruguay in 1813, he received his first mercantile training in the counting house of an English firm in which he early rose to be partner and general manager. Ultimately both at home and in foreign enterprise he became the Brazilian J. P. Morgan of his day, although unlike his North American prototype he ended a bankrupt. Railways, shipyards, drainage canals, an iron foundry, telegraph and telephones, street cars, gold mines, tanneries and textile mills, navigation of the Amazon,[6] a submarine cable to Europe (1874) — nearly every public improvement in the country owned its inception or its encouragement to Barão de Mauá. He dreamed of a vast network of railways and roads uniting the country from the Amazon to the Río de la Plata, extending westward to Paraguay and Bolivia and ultimately to the Pacific — a vision far from realization even today. Mauá became for the time the financial leader of the Atlantic seaboard of South America, an associate of the Rothschilds, owner or part owner of banks in London, New York, Montevideo, and Buenos Aires. He embodied the transition from the routine and

[6] A steamship line whose order, cleanliness, and discipline astonished Louis Agassiz and his wife on their celebrated visit to Brazil in 1865.

traditionalism of a manorial economy to a modern, aggressive capitalism.

Mauá's career has been the subject of much discussion by historians friendly and unfriendly. His relations with the imperial government and with outstanding political figures of his day were close, and as a good banker he often profited from these official contacts. But he was also a man of genuinely constructive idealism, in the midst of the indifference or skepticism of the ruling planter class, in the words of one of his biographers, perhaps "the most notable personality in imperial Brazil." The role of this Brazilian banker was the more remarkable because in the middle of the nineteenth century most industrial and commercial activity in the Empire was in the control of foreigners. Some ten thousand individuals of Portuguese nationality, we are told, monopolized most of the domestic trade, wholesale and retail, while the import and export trade was the peculiar province of the British.

The Emperor himself was to play a somewhat significant, if indirect, part in the attraction of European capital. He made several extended visits to Europe strictly incognito, displaying the inexhaustible curiosity of the zealous tourist, but impressing the practical businessman as well as the statesman and the scholar with his dignity, honesty, simplicity, and wide intellectual interests; and they transferred to his nation the qualities they observed in him. In a sense, Dom Pedro was a sort of imperial broker, unconsciously selling Brazil to the world.

His second voyage to Europe was by way of the United States, on the occasion of the celebration of the centenary of its independence. He spent three months there and covered some 10,000 miles, visiting most of the important cities east of the Mississippi River and penetrating all the way west to the Pacific coast (the first transcontinental railway had been completed less than ten years before). He insisted everywhere that he be treated as a private individual; his curiosity was boundless, his activity indefatigable. As in Europe, he visited schools, museums, factories, hospitals, theaters (including the Chinese theater in San Francisco), newspaper offices, services in churches and synagogues, including the Mormon Temple in Salt Lake City and a Moody and Sankey revival in New York. His presence at the opening of the Centennial Exhibition in Philadelphia in May was the high spot of that occasion. He apparently liked Boston best of all the American cities. Making a lone visit to the Bunker Hill monument at six in the morning, he had to rouse the keeper out of bed, and then finding himself without the fifty-cents admission fee, borrowed a half-dollar from his hack-driver (the keeper did not recognize him). In Cambridge he visited Harvard College, where he was the guest of President Eliot. He was acquainted with most of the New England writers of that era through their works, and had corresponded with a few. He had translated into Portuguese the "Cry of a Lost Soul" by Whittier, whom he made a special effort to meet; and he dined with Emerson, Holmes, and Longfellow at the latter's house on Brattle Street. The United States probably never had a more popular or more sympathetic guest.[7] The increasing volume of Brazilian trade with the United States in the 1870's can be accounted for by other circumstances, especially the growing importance of coffee and rubber, but it is interesting to note that it should more or less coincide with Dom Pedro's visit to the North American republic.

The impact of Brazil's coming of age in the mid-nineteenth century was most evident in relations with adjacent states to the southward. Brazilian capitalist and political penetration between 1850 and 1870 into the basin of the Río de la Plata, in the republics of Uruguay, Argentina, and Paraguay, was

[7] M. W. Williams, *Dom Pedro the Magnanimous* (Chapel Hill, 1937), pp. 186–213.

unmistakable witness of the Empire's growing maturity in contrast with its Spanish neighbors.

As we noted earlier, Portuguese interest in this adjacent region dated from the very beginning of Iberian settlement of the New World, as early as 1530 when Sebastian Cabot returned to Spain after three years spent exploring the banks of the Paraná River. The Portuguese crown, fearful of Spanish intrusion into its territory, organized an expedition under Martim Afonso de Sousa which made the first permanent European settlement in Brazil, São Vicente, today a suburb of the coffee port of Santos. The western limits of Portuguese America had been established by the Treaty of Tordesillas between Spain and Portugal in 1494, only two years after Columbus' first memorable voyage of discovery. But as there was at that time no means of accurately measuring longitude, no one knew just where the line of demarcation lay. The Portuguese preferred to believe that their domain included the estuary of the Río de la Plata. It did not — indeed, not only Uruguay but the present Brazilian states of Santa Catarina and Rio Grande do Sul lay on the Spanish side of the boundary. Consequently this intervening area remained a bone of contention for three hundred years.

Although by treaty in 1777 the Banda Oriental or eastern bank of the Río de la Plata was definitely recognized as a Spanish possession, in the second decade of the nineteenth century, when Dom João VI resided in Brazil, the Portuguese, as already stated, took advantage of quarrels among the Spanish Americans to seize it and annex it to Brazil. A subsequent war with Argentina ended in the erection of an independent buffer republic of Uruguay under the joint protection of its two neighbors. Argentine-Brazilian jealousies in this tiny, embryo republic of 40,000 inhabitants continued, each nation determined to establish its own paramount political influence at the expense of the other; especially as the celebrated dictator of

Buenos Aires, Juan Manuel de Rosas (1835–1852) was believed to be ambitious to restore the territorial unity of the former Spanish viceroyalty by incorporating into Argentina the peripheral republics of Uruguay and Paraguay.

There were, however, other elements in the picture. The vast province of Mato Grosso in the center of Brazil — still today a Brazilian frontier, a semi-tropical region of savanna and scrub-covered upland that sometime may support a large European population — Mato Grosso before the days of the railway was for practical purposes largely inaccessible except by way of the Paraná and Paraguay Rivers. In fact, all the principal rivers of the La Plata system have their sources in Brazil. Peace and free navigation therefore were of vital concern, and friendly governments along the way. And as these governments, in Argentina, Uruguay, and Paraguay, were notoriously unstable — revolution, dictatorship, civil war, seemed endemic — Brazil was always tempted to intervene and ally herself with one party or faction against another, in order to protect her interests. Or at least to create a balance of power in the interest of peace, so that no one strong government, such as that of Rosas, could dominate and perhaps close her line of communications. What was more, in contrast with her unruly neighbors Brazil was a big country, relatively stable and united, with a responsible, representative government that was highly respected abroad. Many of her citizens were residents of Uruguay, and possessed large properties there. They mixed in local politics, and often suffered in their persons and properties in the interminable civil wars in that republic.

In short, the relations of Brazil with the Río de la Plata area bore a close resemblance to those of the United States with the turbulent little republics of Central America and the Caribbean in the first quarter of the present century. Lives and property of our citizens were endangered by incessant revolutions and wars between nations. An important line of our communications, in this case to the Pacific coast via Panama, was menaced unless we maintained our political and military ascendency in that area. We pursued a policy of the Rooseveltian "big stick" — diplomatic intervention, landing of marines — to maintain peace and order and forestall possible intervention by European powers whose nationals had financial and commercial interests there. On the Río de la Plata such European intervention became a reality, and for a decade, from 1838 to 1848, French and English naval squadrons intermittently resorted to "pacific" blockades or actual war, while their diplomats endeavored by negotiation to impose peace between rival parties and the acknowledgment of special privileges for their citizens. In the minds of Brazilian statesmen, as with us, this effort to inflict order and respect for constituted authority on unwilling people was but part of "the white man's burden," a civilizing action of their diplomacy, their right and duty as one of the first powers of America.

The policies of the imperial government on the Río de la Plata resulted in two foreign wars during the reign of Dom Pedro II. In one Brazil helped overthrow the Argentine dictator Rosas, in 1851–52, in alliance with the government in Uruguay and the opposition party in Argentina. The other, the celebrated war against Paraguay in 1865–1870, was waged to eliminate the notorious Paraguayan dictator, Francisco Solano López. Again it was a triple alliance, of Brazil, Argentina, and Uruguay, a war in which Brazil supplied most of the men, money, and armament, and acquired a war debt that hampered Dom Pedro's government for years thereafter.

The earlier war against Rosas concerned the balance of power on the great river system. As among the republics of Central America, Argentina and Uruguay were too close neighbors not to be mixed up in one another's politics. Whether in Central or in South America, the political opposition in one country always found across the frontier aid and comfort from friends and sympathizers, or asylum in time of need. Domestic politics were at the same time international politics. The Argentine dictator gave military aid to the Blancos, one of the contending groups across the river. The rival, Colorado, faction, led by Fructuoso Rivera and in possession of Montevideo, retorted by harboring the enemies of Rosas or supporting them at home. The outcome was a long and desultory war between the Argentine dictator and the government in Montevideo. This city was invested on the land side for over eight years (1843–1851), and hence called by Alexandre Dumas the "New Troy." At the same time Rosas closed the Paraná River to all maritime traffic, in order to hamper his foes in the Argentine provinces and Paraguay up the river valley. As he was thought to be aiming to absorb both Uruguay and Paraguay into the Argentine confederation,[8] one might well believe that the balance of power was at stake.

Persuaded of this were also the governments of France and England, which represented large mercantile interests in that area, interests that suffered from the endless disorders. They allied themselves with Rivera and the Argentine exiles, and in 1845 instituted a naval blockade of Argentine shores,[9] while the little republic of Uruguay survived only by the grace of its two European protectors. The defense of the city of Montevideo was largely the work of foreign residents, to which Garibaldi, retiring from the republican revolt in Rio Grande do Sul, contributed with his Italian Legion. In 1847–48 the British, and then the French, for a variety of reasons withdrew

[8] When Brazil by treaty in 1844 formally recognized the independence of Paraguay, Buenos Aires immediately protested. And in 1850 Rosas was authorized by his Buenos Aires legislature to employ measures of every sort to make effective the reincorporation of the "province" of Paraguay into the Argentine confederation.

[9] The French government in an earlier dispute with Rosas had maintained for two and a half years (1838–1840) a blockade of Buenos Aires.

their fleets from the river and their subsidies from the regime in Montevideo, although peace was not formally achieved until two years later.

The imperial government in Rio de Janeiro had followed with close attention, and some concern, these developments on the Río de la Plata, the more so as at times they were involved in the rebellion of the *gaúchos* in Rio Grande do Sul. Brazilian emissaries were active in Paraguay and Corrientes, in Uruguay and in London. A proposal to Brazil by Rosas in 1843 for an offensive-defensive alliance, in the face of threatened Anglo-French intervention, was accepted, but after the treaty was ratified by the Emperor, Rosas, the danger seemingly past, refused his confirmation — which was interpreted by Brazil as a gratuitous affront.[10] A mission of the Visconde de Abrantes to Europe in 1844 to urge joint intervention by Brazil, France, and England to save Uruguay's independence, was unsuccessful. Intervention by England and France alone materialized in the following year, but their eventual withdrawal without securing any of their objectives left Rosas apparently triumphant throughout the great river valley. If Uruguay's independence was to be preserved, Brazil must step in to fill the breach. In 1851–52, after many diplomatic preliminaries, the imperial government combined with the domestic foes of Rosas and with the Colorado Party in Montevideo, first to raise the long siege of that city, and then to overthrow the Argentine dictator at home.[11] By his defeat at the Battle of Monte Caseros on February 3, 1852, Rosas was eliminated from the American scene (to survive another twenty-five years as an obscure country gentleman in England), and Argentina was enabled to take her first faltering steps toward national organization.

Brazil in other ways proceeded to consolidate her position in

[10] Calógeras, *Formação histórica do Brasil*, pp. 243–244.
[11] In becoming a party to the Alliance of May 29, 1851, Brazil gave as a reason efforts made by Rosas and his allies to separate the province of Rio Grande do Sul from the Empire.

La Plata politics. While the triple alliance was being negotiated, the imperial government took advantage of Uruguay's
extreme weakness to impose a treaty recognizing the Brazilian
interpretation of the boundary line separating the two countries. And after the expulsion of Rosas, its political interest
in Uruguayan affairs continued to be uncomfortably close. In
1854, at the request of the Colorado President Flores, Brazil
sent 4000 troops to help maintain the government against its
Blanco foes, and they remained there for nearly two years —
much like North American marines in Nicaragua in the 1920's.

The spearhead of economic penetration, "the most powerful diplomatic agency of the Empire," was Barão de Mauá.
As early as 1850, after the withdrawal of England and France,
he had been called in by the Brazilian Minister of Finance to
provide secret monthly subsidies (12,000 pesos) to the be-
leaguered Montevideo government. And he had apparently
played an important role in the arming and outfitting of the
forces contributed to the joint campaign against Rosas. After
the latter's defeat, Mauá continued his association with the
Río de la Plata, establishing branches of his bank,[12] becoming
the chief fiscal agent of the Uruguayan regime, and the most
effective medium for the financial and industrial rehabilitation
of the tiny prostrate nation. It was largely Brazilian capital,
especially that of Mauá, that in following years was active in
the promotion of railways and telegraphs, of illuminating gas
in the capital and other new enterprises, and in the revival and
improvement of the cattle industry on which Uruguay today
still depends.[13] In fact, it was this deep involvement in trade
and industry, and especially in government finance, in Uruguay that helped to bring about the second war, against Paraguay, and ultimately a decade later the failure of the Mauá

[12] In Montevideo the Banco Mauá y Cia. (1857), the first important bank
in Uruguay.
[13] The famous Compañía Pastoril, Agricola y Industrial with large *estancias*
in Uruguay and Argentina.

Bank. During these years Mauá's financial interests were almost equally important across the Río de la Plata, in the business and confused politics of the Argentine Republic.

The Paraguayan War, one of the two great international wars of the nineteenth century in South America, which lasted for five years and in which Brazil was the chief protagonist, had a confused and confusing background. It again grew out of the alliance of antagonistic parties in Argentina with warring factions in Uruguay, grew also out of the involvement of Brazilian cattle barons of Rio Grande in revolutionary activities across the border, and their harassment in turn by the government in Montevideo. The Colorado leader, Venancio Flores, was again in revolt in 1863, joined by Brazilians on both sides of the frontier, and the Blanco authorities in Montevideo accused both Buenos Aires and Rio de Janeiro of collusion. To all this was added, for good measure, the overweening ambition of a *mestizo* dictator of Paraguay, Francisco Solano López, with a Napoleonic complex conceived in Paraguay and nurtured in Paris, to dictate international policies on the Río de la Plata.[14]

The imperial government was in an awkward situation. Brazilian subjects and property were among the chief sufferers in the political commotions in Uruguay. The government had a long list of grievances, and diplomatic protests brought little or no satisfaction. It had to try and protect Brazilian interests, and at the same time restrain the Riograndenses, keep them from retaliating — yet not alienate them, a people traditionally

[14] Paraguay, the oldest Spanish community on the Atlantic slopes of South America, in the nineteenth century was still a rather primitive, isolated agrarian society, ruled by a succession of autocratic presidents, although notoriously turbulent and with a fine sense of its independence. Boundary disputes with both Argentina and Brazil served to complicate its international relations. The population was, and is, mostly *mestizo*, with a large proportion of Guaraní blood. And although Spanish is the language of government and society, Guaraní is the common tongue even in households of the educated.

impatient of control from Rio de Janeiro. Wearied of civil strife across the border, it finally yielded to the importunities of the Riograndense leaders. Early in 1864 the younger, more aggressive, interventionist elements in the Brazilian Chamber gained the upper hand; and after the failure of efforts by both Rio and Buenos Aires to bring about an adjustment, the Brazilian envoy, supported by a naval squadron off the coast, presented on August 4, 1864 an ultimatum to Montevideo: restoration of domestic peace and redress of grievances, or military reprisals. The Blanco president, who in turn had been cultivating an alliance with López of Paraguay,[15] trusting to support from that direction and from the provincial party in Argentina hostile to the Buenos Aires administration, assumed a defiant attitude. And in September orders were issued to Brazilian troops to cross the border. An alliance was soon negotiated with the Colorado rebels, and in the following February, 1865, Montevideo was captured and the Colorado Party established in control.

The invasion of Uruguay brought President López into the conflict. At the end of the preceding August he had addressed a famous protest to the Brazilian emperor through the minister in Asunción: keep hands off Uruguay — let no one disturb the balance of power on the Río de la Plata! Dom Pedro rejected the protest, and on receiving news of the Brazilian invasion López began hostilities against Brazil. In November he seized a Brazilian steamer carrying a new provincial president and official remittances up the Paraguay River to Mato Grosso, and in December proceeded to take possession of disputed territory in that province.

López at the same time demanded of President Mitre in Buenos Aires permission to cross the Argentine province of Corrientes in order to attack Brazil in the south. This was

[15] Both Brazil and Argentina were on bad terms with López because of boundary disputes, and feared and respected him because of his large army.

refused; so in March 1865 he declared war on Argentina and invaded the province. This violation of Argentine soil enabled Mitre to unite temporarily the discordant elements in the nation, and even to join in a military alliance with Brazil and the new government in Uruguay, both of which the Argentine provincials cordially hated. The resultant conflict was consequently known in contemporary newspapers as the War of the Triple Alliance. The Allies agreed not to make peace until the firebrand López was eliminated, the fortifications of Paraguay demolished, its army disbanded, indemnities exacted, and boundaries imposed acceptable to them — terms uncomfortably reminiscent of the aims of the Allies against the Central Powers in the First World War in 1914.

Into the military details of this long and disastrous war we need not enter. Paraguay occupied a superb strategic position: a compact little country, centrally located, surrounded by rivers. President López had created an army of over 60,000 men, fairly well drilled and disciplined, though with antiquated muskets and artillery, the greatest military force South America had ever seen, and regarded as a menace by its neighbors. The combined military establishments of Brazil and Argentina were much smaller.

For the Allies the war was not a brilliant military achievement: they suffered from mediocre generalship, lack of adequate maps and plans of the terrain fought over, commissariat and hospital services wretchedly organized. Their armies sustained terrific losses from heat, fever, and insects in tropical swamps and forests. With the prolongation of the war, the initial patriotic enthusiasm cooled, and extraordinary measures had to be taken to replace losses from battle and disease. Also the war was not popular in the Argentine interior, and twice there were provincial revolts to try and force a peace.

An initial Paraguayan drive down the valley of the Uruguay River to divide the Allies and seize Rio Grande do Sul miscarried, and at the siege and capture of the invading forces at Uruguayana Dom Pedro himself was in nominal command. The first army of López was virtually destroyed. Yet not until April 1866 were the Allies prepared to invade Paraguay itself. In 1867 President Mitre, who had ranked as supreme commander, was recalled to restore order at home, and replaced by an abler strategist, the Marquês de Caxias; and it was only in July 1868 that the Allied armies finally forced their way past the formidable defenses of Humaitá on the Paraguay River (the Sebastopol of the war) on the road to Asunción. A second line established by López at Angostura was outflanked by Caxias, and by the end of the year in a series of blows the bulk of the Paraguayan army was dispersed. On January 5, 1869, the Allies entered the Paraguayan capital. Caxias, old, tired, and in ill-health, then turned in his resignation, and was replaced in March by the Emperor's son-in-law, the Conde d'Eu. Eight months later the Allies signed a preliminary treaty of peace with a provisional government they had set up in Asunción.

For Paraguay it was a war of attrition. When the able-bodied men gave out, López summoned the old men, boys, women, and girls to take their places. And they fought with amazing courage and tenacity. López was defeated less by military failure than by disease and starvation. Before the Allied advance, he fled into the wilds of the north, dragging after him the remnants of an army and masses of fugitives, until brought to bay at Cerro Corá on March 1, 1870, and killed by a cavalryman's lance. "He had sworn to die for his country, and he did, though his country might perish with him."

Probably no nation in modern times has come so close to annihilation as Paraguay. Its towns and fields were devastated, its industry ruined. Some 200,000 fought in the war, out of a population of perhaps less than a million. Nearly all the able-bodied men were killed, and thousands died of starvation and disease. At the end, women over fifteen outnumbered the men more than four to one. Polygamy was the inevitable consequence. Women owned and managed the farms and ranches, did the manual labor, became the breadwinners. Yet today Francisco Solano López is preëminently the national hero of Paraguay. He was a ruthless dictator, vain, capricious, arrogant, absolutely without scruple, and at times ferociously cruel; who treated everyone's property as his own, executed, banished, or imprisoned anyone he thought too influential, even members of his own family. But he was intensely jealous of the independence of his country, which he identified with himself, and over the mass of the people he exerted an extraordinary hypnotic power. To them he was the "Great Father," who talked to them in their own language of Guaraní, the invincible champion, the greatest ruler in the world.[16]

During the war Dom Pedro was much criticized for continuing the conflict to the bitter end, to the death of López and the virtual extinction of the republic. At one moment, in 1867, López had offered to demolish the defenses of the country, admit free navigation of the rivers, accept the frontiers imposed by the Allies, and pay the expenses of the war. But eliminate himself from the scene he refused to do. Although some in the Brazilian ministry favored ending the war by negotiation, the Emperor in spite of occasional moments of uncertainty refused to compromise. He was no pacifist. He might regard López as a disturber of continental peace and a scourge of civilized society, but he also called the war "um bom choque elétrico a nacionalidade." Of the Allies, Brazil was the chief sufferer from the war, in dead and disabled, in

[16] W. R. Shepherd, *The Hispanic Nations of the New World* (New Haven, 1919), pp. 94, 99.

public indebtedness and deferment of material improvement. Dom Pedro himself showed the effects of his long and unceasing responsibilities and emerged a man much older for his years.

After 1870 Paraguay was weighed down with millions in indemnities exacted by the victors which the nation could never hope to liquidate. Argentine and Uruguayan troops were immediately withdrawn, but Brazil kept there for several years an army of occupation of 14,000 men to insure public order. The war indemnities one by one were ultimately canceled. In recent times Paraguay has become to all intents and purposes an economic dependency of Argentina, and only the huge shadow of Brazil has insured its political independence.

One of the casualties of the Paraguayan War was the Mauá Bank. The chief financial power in Uruguay in the 1860's, and unfettered by the bitter partisanship of that tumultuous republic of less than a quarter-million inhabitants, it nevertheless fell victim to the frequent and violent changes of government in Montevideo. The fiscal agent of the Blanco administration before 1865, it also loyally supported the Colorado regime installed by Brazilian arms in that year. But gratitude of the Colorados was soon replaced by an increasing nationalist resentment against submission to foreign political and economic tutelage. This ill-will was directed especially against foreign banks of issue, and by a series of measures the Mauá Bank was twice obliged to close its doors, in 1868 and in 1869. In Brazil itself the war had forced resort to extensive foreign loans and large issues of paper money, and a consequent policy of deflation after the conflict undermined the solvency of many of the banks. In May 1875 the Mauá Bank suspended payments, and in its liquidation during the next three years Visconde de Mauá was stripped of all his possessions. A loan of 7000 contos by the government might have saved

the bank, except for the bitter, partisan opposition headed by
Zacarias de Góes e Vasconcelos. In 1878 the creditors received
65 per cent of their claims, and on complete settlement in 1882
over 90 per cent. Mauá died in Petrópolis in October 1889,
eighteen days before the fall of the Empire with whose
material welfare he had been so closely associated.

Chapter Five

* * * * * * * * * * * * *

THE SLAVERY QUESTION

One unfortunate legacy of the Brazilian Empire from colonial times was the institution of African slavery. It became more and more "an anomaly in a country governed by an Emperor renowned for his liberal and humanitarian views," and it proved ultimately to be one of the causes of the Empire's collapse. Brazil was also until the middle of the nineteenth century one of the few countries of Western culture that acquiesced in the slave trade with Africa. The last twenty years of the Empire witnessed a growing determination of the majority of Brazilians to remove the stigma of Negro bondage from the nation's good name.[1] The bitter and long-drawn-out Civil War in the United States was an object lesson of something to be avoided at all costs. Especially after 1863 emancipation became a problem that shook Brazilian society to its depths.

Negro slavery was introduced into Brazil with the commencement of European immigration and settlement in the first half of the sixteenth century. There was Indian slavery too in the beginning, which persisted long in the southern

[1] In the Spanish American republics chattel slavery, although of decreasing importance, had everywhere been abolished by the 1850's, in response to a resurgence of liberalism largely inspired by the revolutions of 1848 in Europe.

provinces and became one of the sources of conflict between Portuguese and Spaniards in that region. But in the northeast, in the area of Pernambuco and Bahia, where there rapidly developed a plantation, sugar-cane economy, the Indian was soon replaced by the Negro. The initial cost of the imported African was greater, but he had a stronger physique, was more intelligent and docile, and withstood more easily hard labor in the tropics. Already by 1585 Pernambuco was reported to have some ten thousand African slaves, many times outnumbering the Europeans, and Bahia between three and four thousand. And that area remains today the "black belt" of Brazil, somewhat like parts of our own deep South.

For over a hundred years Brazil supplied most of the sugar to European markets, until the rise of competing plantations in the West Indies in the eighteenth century. And Pernambuco was notorious for the wealth, ostentation, and tropical relaxation of manners of its sugar planters. With the spectacular rise of gold and diamond mining in Minas Gerais in the eighteenth century, and the later rapid expansion of coffee culture in the provinces of Rio de Janeiro, Minas Gerais, and São Paulo, the number of Negroes greatly increased in these south-central areas as well, so that under the Empire Negro slaves had come to represent an immense property investment. Of the estimated population of between seven and eight million in 1845, perhaps a third were slaves.

Foreign visitors to Brazil in the nineteenth century generally agree that treatment of the slaves was relatively mild. Sadistic masters and mulatto overseers were of course not unknown, and as elsewhere long hours of labor, insufficient food and shelter, and cruel corporal punishments often made the lot of the African slaves a hopelessly bitter one. After the supply from abroad dried up with the abolition of the slave trade, prices advanced, the slave became more valuable, and treatment generally more humane. That suicide and infanticide were common, as has been charged, may be questioned, and some foreign observers compared favorably the life of the Brazilian slave in a benign climate with that of the factory worker in contemporary England. In any case, the institution was often mitigated by the humanity, charity, and often generosity of the Portuguese temperament. There was no Code Noir such as prevailed in the French and English West Indies. The Negro was accepted as a member of the human race. Within the Christian community the African slave had his black saints, his religious fraternities and festivals, associations rarely possible in our own ante-bellum South. His right to possess property was recognized by law. A good slave was often freed by bequest of his master or mistress; or he might accumulate, with his master's permission or assistance, enough to purchase his freedom, often at half or less of his legal value. Once free, he encountered no sharp color line; much depended on native ability. As the African woman possessed a peculiar fascination for the white Portuguese man, miscegenation was common from earliest times. There was therefore a numerous class of half-breeds of various shades of brown (*pardos*) included in the free population.[2] The imported Africans, moreover, especially those from the Sudan, were not savages. They possessed an important culture of their own, and in the practical arts of husbandry and craftsmanship often had something to teach to their Portuguese masters. This influence survives, not only in the Brazilian vocabulary and modes of speech, but in many national customs today.

All of these circumstances served to attenuate the color prejudice. The physical type was never an obstacle to amicable and harmonious relations between Portuguese and the free Negroes and mulattoes. Among the statesmen of the Empire were men of color, and several were enobled by the

---

[2] The *mameluco*, offspring of the European and the Indian, was more typical of the pastoral regions of the interior and the extreme south.

Crown. Abolition therefore left no inheritance of racial hatred between whites and blacks, or between mulattoes and Negroes, an immense advantage that Brazil has continued to enjoy down to the present day.[3] Nevertheless, as Brazil was an almost wholly agricultural country, whose plantation economy rested on slave labor, abolition presented an extremely complex problem. Distinguished and far-sighted Brazilians had advocated emancipation from the first days of the Empire, notably José Bonifácio de Andrada and Diogo Antônio Feijó, but it required half a century to mature the liberation sentiment throughout the nation, and gradually to overcome the stubborn opposition of those whose social and economic interests were bound up with the slavery institution.

There were two facets to the slavery question. One was the slave trade from Africa, essential as a provider of the system, for the slave population was not self-perpetuating. Men outnumbered the women, the slave woman was not prolific, and the mortality rate was high. The other was the institution itself. And the problem that first arose was that of the slave trade, which was closely tied to relations with Great Britain. In fact, it was a principal factor in the decline of

[3] Not that Brazil has attained to complete social and economic equality of the races today. Many families of the *alta sociedade* are jealous of their racial purity, although older, historic families will admit to some Indian or African ancestors in the very distant past. And men and women of color who have achieved intellectual and social graces are accepted on terms of equality. In theaters, hotels, and other public places the color prejudice is nonexistent. As in other modern societies, social discrimination has largely an economic basis. In the middle and lower classes, marriage between whites and persons of color is not uncommon, nor is it a matter of public comment. And for historic reasons, the "hewers of wood and drawers of water" are most of them black Africans. When the writer was in Brazil in 1950, Katherine Dunham, a woman of personal charm and artistic and intellectual distinction, was refused accommodations by a well-known hotel of São Paulo on the plea that no rooms were available. It created a national scandal, for the belief was general that the hotel management was moved by consideration for the prejudices of its North American clientele. The newspapers rose in their wrath to denounce the management, and the state legislature enacted a law making such incidents more difficult in the future.

British political and economic ascendency enjoyed since the beginning of the century.

Agitation in England for the abolition of human slavery and the slave trade, with which the great name of William Wilberforce is chiefly associated, resulted in Parliament's abolition of the traffic by an Act of 1807. Thereafter Great Britain, relying on its naval and mercantile supremacy throughout the world, brought increasing pressure to bear on other nations, by treaty or other means, to do likewise. The Lord Strangford Treaty of 1810, which granted special privileges to English trade with Brazil,[4] also provided that the Portuguese would not engage in the slave trade from non-Portuguese parts of Africa. And this was but the first of a series of restrictive agreements to which the government in Brazil was constrained to agree. By a treaty of 1815 the slave trade north of the Equator was forbidden. Two years later Dom João VI promised to limit the importation of slaves to Portuguese subjects, recognized the right of search by British cruisers, and agreed to the creation of two mixed claims commissions, one in Rio de Janeiro, the other in Sierra Leone, to adjudicate cases arising out of seizures. These international engagements, so far as the Brazilians were concerned, remained on paper only. Opposition in Brazil was so great that the crown was powerless to enforce them; nor did the government possess the naval forces needed effectively to police the coasts.

England's role in securing Portugal's recognition of Brazilian independence by the treaty of 1825 gave her another opportunity to present a bill for services rendered. It was acknowledged in the form of two more conventions, one in 1826 in which Brazil promised the total abolition of the slave trade three years after ratification. Thereafter it would be treated as piracy. The other convention, in 1827, renewed for

[4] Also the right of British residents in Brazil to be tried by their own consular courts, for many years a source of bitterness and irritation.

fifteen years Britain's special commercial privileges. To achieve ratification of the Convention of 1826 Britain really forced Dom Pedro I to fall back on his personal powers and defy public opinion. It occasioned the first serious conflict between the new Parliament and the Emperor, thereby jeopardizing the stability of the monarchy. It was only after Dom Pedro's abdication that the triumphant Liberals in Parliament passed an act to enforce the promise given five years before. All slaves imported thereafter, with few exceptions, were by law automatically free.

But the law could not be enforced. The importation of Negroes increased, especially with the spread of coffee plantations. The treaties only caused hatred of Great Britain and even minor outbreaks against the government. Traders were abetted and protected by the planters, whose prosperity and wealth were measured by the number of their slaves. Government orders were either disobeyed by the local authorities or carried out with such ill-will or lack of zeal that they were of no effect. It is a striking fact that most of the contraband Negroes were landed on the coast in the vicinity of Rio de Janeiro between Cape Frio and Santos, and even within the Bay of Rio itself. The British attributed this noncompliance with the treaty to the duplicity or bad faith of the imperial authorities; and since to a very real degree the planter aristocracy was the government, the charge at times was doubtless not without some foundation. On the other hand, indemnifications decreed by the mixed commissions for ships illegally seized by British cruisers were not paid by the British, and repeated demands by the Brazilian government met with no response.

It also appears that ships and ship-captains engaged in the trade represented mostly capital of Portuguese origin,[5] the vast profits accruing to it while the odium remained with Brazil,

[5] Calógeras, *Formação histórica*, pp. 228–229.

a circumstance ultimately borne in upon the Brazilians themselves. The large fortunes arising out of the trade constituted
a sinister financial power that stopped at nothing to defend
its interests, "subsidizing journals, bribing officials [and]
stimulating by every means the political or police persecution
of its adversaries." [6] It has been calculated that during the
decade 1840–1850 over 368,000 Africans were imported,
representing some 373,000 contos of reis, or over 40,000,000
sterling,[7] and Anglo-Brazilian relations grew steadily worse.

When in 1844 the commercial treaty lapsed, Great Britain
was unable to secure another even on terms of equality with
other nations. When in the following year the Convention of
1826, which as in 1817 admitted the right of search by British
cruisers and continued the mixed claims commissions, also
expired, and the Brazilian government refused renewal, Britain retorted with the Aberdeen Act of August 1845, authoriz-
ing the condemnation of foreign slave ships by British ad-
miralty courts. British cruisers apparently had often pursued
slavers into Brazilian territorial waters, and even landed
marines. This new affront to national sovereignty provoked
an explosion of patriotic wrath against British "aggression,"
the effect of which was to stimulate the trade to an unprecedented volume. Whereas in the early forties the Negroes
introduced annually numbered some 20,000 or less, in 1846
the figure rose to over 50,000, and in 1848 to 60,000.[8]

In September 1848, a Conservative ministry came into
power determined to put an end to a discreditable situation,
and prepared a law that effectively deterred the slavers. But
even this might have failed of parliamentary approval had not

[6] Sérgio Buarque de Holanda, *Raízes do Brasil*, p. 93.

[7] Maurício Goulart, *Escravidão africana no Brasil* (2nd ed., São Paulo,
1950), p. 270.

[8] Calógeras, *Formação histórica*, pp. 272–273; Alan K. Manchester, *British
Preëminence in Brazil, Its Rise and Decline* (Chapel Hill, 1933), pp. 285ff.

the British ministry in the middle of 1850 issued formal orders to its cruisers to enter Brazilian territorial waters and harbors to make captures.[9] The Eusebio de Queiroz Law, named after its author, was finally sanctioned in September 1850. In 1851 the importations of Negroes fell to little more than 3000, and to 700 in 1852. English ships and Brazilian authorities now worked together to eliminate the slavers. The same result would doubtless have been achieved without the extreme British pressure. The increasing strength and stability of the imperial government after 1840, and especially after the suppression of the Pernambuco revolt in 1848, and the gradual growth of an enlightened public opinion, enabled the crown to accomplish what many circumstances in the nation had earlier rendered impossible.

The ultimate benefits to Brazil were of an economic and material order as well as moral. Immense sums were no longer withdrawn from agriculture to pay for slaves. Luzo-Brazilian capital normally invested in the slave trade, as stated earlier, was immobilized and soon diverted into industrial activities and the establishment of institutions of credit necessary for the activation of economic enterprise. But the conflict also left a legacy of bad feeling that beclouded Anglo-Brazilian relations for many years thereafter. And popular anti-British resentment was renewed in the 1860's by an unfortunate diplomatic quarrel known as the "Christie Affair."

A British vessel wrecked on the shores of Rio Grande do Sul in June 1861 had apparently been plundered by natives, and the Brazilian authorities had been slow in bringing the guilty to justice. Shortly after, three sailors not in uniform from a British war vessel had been arrested in Rio de Janeiro for disorderly conduct, but were released as soon as their

[9] Between August 1849 and May 1851, as reported by the Ministry of Foreign Affairs in the latter year, ninety slave ships were "captured, destroyed and condemned" by British cruisers. Goulart, *Escravidão africana,* p. 259.

identity was established. The British minister, W. D. Christie, tactless and self-assertive, unfriendly to Brazil, had taken a high hand from the start; and the British cabinet, accepting his version of the incidents, demanded on pain of reprisals an apology from the imperial government, punishment of all involved in the arrest and imprisonment of the sailors, and restitution and damages in the case of the shipwrecked vessel. When the Brazilian foreign minister demurred, British warships blockaded Rio de Janeiro for six days, until the Brazilian government agreed to pay the damages demanded and to arbitrate the case of the arrests. But later the government in turn demanded an expression of regret and compensation for the seizure of Brazilian vessels during the blockade. Upon Britain's refusal, in June 1863 Brazil severed diplomatic relations. Although Great Britain ultimately offered to apologize for the blockade, but without compensation, diplomatic relations were not resumed until the outbreak of the Paraguayan War. During the siege of Uruguayana in 1865 the Emperor accepted apologies tendered by the British minister to the Río de la Plata, Sir Edward Thornton, waiving the claim for damages, and amicable relations were restored.

The Paraguayan War kept the consideration of social problems, such as Negro slavery, for the time being more or less in abeyance, but its influence upon the political evolution of the Empire was considerable. The Moderating Power of the Emperor, which under the Constitution served to harmonize or check partisan struggles in an imperfect parliamentary system, was for the first time seriously called into question. Resort to this power, especially in bringing about cabinet changes or alternation of parties in the government, invariably led to criticism by the parliamentary opposition, although these same individuals were quick enough to appeal to the Emperor to exercise his personal powers, when occasion warranted, in their own behalf. Consequently the crown, presumably above all parties, was increasingly exposed to violent partisan attacks. Dom Pedro, although he had no favorites and few confidants, attending to and respecting all opinions, also harbored no resentments. Insults and calumnies he tolerated with philosophical detachment; and since he never defended himself in public, his apparent unconcern only served to irritate his foes.[10]

After 1848 the Conservative ascendency in the government had continued for over a decade, although in 1853 Carneiro Leão, Marquês de Paraná, succeeded in organizing the celebrated Conciliation which survived his death three years later. After 1862 the cabinets displayed increasing liberal tendencies, culminating in the ministry of Zacarias de Góes e Vasconcelos in 1866–1868. The fall of this ministry in the midst of the Paraguayan War involved a political crisis that was ultimately to have a profound effect upon the fortunes of the monarchy. Zacarias and the more radical elements among the Liberals were convinced of the necessity of emancipating the Negro. Antislavery sentiment generally was slowly increasing, and occasional voices were raised in Parliament and in the press, but positive action was postponed by the war. Apart from the financial burdens involved, it was felt important to avoid controversies as much as possible, maintain national solidarity as long as the conflict lasted. Moreover, the belief was still general that Negro slavery was basic in the Brazilian economy, and to uproot it suddenly would entail disastrous results. However, during the war state-owned slaves, and some privately owned, who offered to enlist in the army were declared free, and about 6000 thereby won their liberty. And near its close, the Conde d'Eu, then commanding the Allied forces, induced the Provisional Government set up in Asunción to proclaim the freedom of slaves in Paraguay.

Dom Pedro throughout his lifetime had been opposed to slavery and threw his influence on the side of abolition. As

[10] Calógeras, *Formação histórica*, pp. 335–336.

far back as 1840, the year of his formal "majority," he had set an example by freeing all the slaves he had inherited as his personal property. But the supply of free labor was very limited, and the plantation system, whether of sugar, cotton, or coffee, requiring a large labor force, depended on Negro bondage. So the Emperor favored a gradual, carefully planned, abolition, and he was careful not to move too fast in advance of public opinion. He hoped for a program that would respect property rights of the slave owners and not seriously disrupt agriculture. As early as 1865 he requested an eminent lawyer, Pimenta Bueno, later Marquês de São Vicente, to prepare a project for progressive emancipation; and in 1867, partly as a result of his prodding, a commission of the Council of State was appointed to frame a law, headed by one of the most distinguished political personalities of the time, José Thomaz Nabuco de Araújo. In the Speech from the Throne of the same year, and again in 1868, the government for the first time dared refer publicly to the imminence of Negro emancipation.

It was a Conservative government, however, that was to put through Parliament the first statute aiming at eventual abolition. In July 1868 the Zacarias ministry fell over a question of constitutional procedure concerning the selection of a senator to fill a vacancy created by the death of a Liberal from the province of Rio Grande do Norte. Of the three nominees elected by the province, the Council of State chose a Conservative; the cabinet wanted a Liberal who, as it happened, had also received the greatest number of electoral votes. Zacarias protested to the Emperor, who refused to disregard the Council's advice. The ministry therefore resigned. Dom Pedro reluctantly agreed, and asked a Conservative, the Visconde de Itaboraí, wealthy planter and senator from the province of Rio de Janeiro, to form a new government.

The slavery question was involved, for Zacarias wished to

maintain the strength of the antislavery forces in the upper house. But the fundamental issue was constitutional. The appointing power rested in the Emperor, in consultation with the Council of State, not in the cabinet; and although no law clearly required that he follow the Council's advice, that had long been the practice. Zacarias, some surmise, may have raised the issue as a covert attack on the Moderating Power itself, which many Liberals believed should reside in the ministry. In the Council Conservative influences predominated, and Zacarias may have thought that no progress toward emancipation was possible so long as it played a decisive role in the government.[11] On the other hand, Dom Pedro may have felt that so long as the war lasted the direction of affairs was safer in Conservative hands. The Liberal majority in the Chamber chose to regard this as a *coup d'état,* and exploited it to the utmost, branding it as Machiavellian astuteness, despotism, and so on. As the Chamber promptly passed a sharp vote of lack of confidence in the new ministry, the Emperor dissolved it and called for a general election, which of course returned a government, that is, a Conservative, majority. Therafter, however, Dom Pedro always followed the wishes of the cabinet in the selection of senators.

A consequence of the so-called *coup d'état* of 1868 was that the Liberals, who had been split into several factions, emerged for the moment as a single radical, almost antidynastic, group. And in manifestoes of May and November, 1869, they announced a far-reaching program of reform, much the same and quite as comprehensive as what the radicals demanded forty years earlier when they forced the abdication of Dom Pedro I. The program called for the abolition of the Moderating Power, the Council of State, the National Guard (through its officers a citadel of privilege), and human slavery. In more concrete terms it demanded direct elections and wide-

[11] J. M. dos Santos, *A política geral do Brasil* (São Paulo, 1930), pp. 108–109.

spread suffrage; senators elected for a limited term; popular election of provincial governors, magistrates, and other local officials; an independent judiciary; complete religious liberty; and freedom of education and of association.[12]

This radical pronouncement of 1869 envisaged a complete decentralization of government. It was a synthesis of everything the democratic and federalistic forces in the nation had stood for since the founding of the Empire. In fact, as someone has said, the constitution would not be reformed, it would be a new constitution foreshadowing a republic. This program remained the lodestar of the reformers throughout the next two decades and generated a current of public opinion to which the Conservatives were progressively forced to do homage. After 1868 successive Conservative cabinets held out until the ministry of Silva Paranhos, Visconde de Rio Branco, came into power in March 1871 prepared to revive the slavery issue. Following terrific oratorical battles in Parliament, a law based on Nabuco's project of three years earlier was passed in September during the Emperor's absence in Europe, the Rio Branco Law or "Law of Free Birth."

All children of slaves born thereafter were free, but they were apprenticed to the mother's owner until the age of twenty-one, or they might be released at the age of eight for an indemnity paid by the government. The law provided for the accumulation of redemption funds by local communities, as a natural corollary required the registration of all slaves and their children, and declared free the slaves belonging to the state or to the crown. It did anticipate gradual abolition in the course of nature, but very gradual; apparently it got by the slavocrats only as a compromise, to put off the evil day of total abolition as long as possible. And as a matter of fact, the redemption funds seem to have been little used.

The Law of Free Birth, although sponsored by the Liberals,

[12] *Ibid.*, pp. 123–125.

was put through by the Conservatives, and for a half-dozen years thereafter the question of abolition remained more or less quiescent, so long as the Conservatives remained in power. But meanwhile a strong movement of opinion was gaining headway for a reform of the electoral system, chiefly elicited by the Liberals; and in January 1878 Dom Pedro seized the occasion of the retirement of the aged and ailing Duque de Caxias as head of the cabinet to invite the Liberals to form a government. The Chamber was dissolved, and in the ensuing election the Liberals were returned with a strong majority. With them appeared new names and new ideas. Among their most eminent leaders was Joaquim Nabuco,[13] young, eloquent, talented, in the forefront of the abolitionist campaign, and ably seconded by outstanding personalities of African descent, notably André Rebouças, and the journalist from São Paulo, José de Patrocínio, of great eloquence and literary powers.

The Law of Free Birth as a compromise never satisfied the abolitionists. In 1880 and later prominent citizens organized antislavery societies which in 1883 united in the Abolitionist Confederation. The provincial assemblies of São Paulo, Minas Gerais, and Rio de Janeiro imposed prohibitive taxes on the caravans of slaves introduced from other provinces into this great coffee-growing area. In 1884 the northern provinces of Ceará and Amazonas by local option emancipated all slaves within their borders, as later in the year did many of the towns in Rio Grande do Sul. Some of the progressive planters were doing so privately on their estates, especially in the province of São Paulo.[14] Among private individuals the most notable

[13] He later wrote a brilliant life of his father, José Nabuco de Araújo, *Um Estadista do Império*, today a Brazilian classic, and subsequently was ambassador in Washington under the Republic.

[14] Mauá, always an abolitionist, had liberated his slaves as far back as the 1840's, and in 1866 the celebrated Benedictine Monastery in Rio de Janeiro had emancipated 1,600 of its Negroes.

was a wealthy coffee planter of Portuguese birth, Nicolau de Campos Vergueiro, prominent in Liberal ranks ever since the first days of the Regency and later an imperial senator. In 1846 Snr. Vergueiro began bringing families of white laborers from Europe to his estates in São Paulo, on a contractual basis, chiefly from German Switzerland. The proprietor advanced transportation costs, provided a house and furnished provisions, clothes, and tools at wholesale prices. The colonist undertook to tend so many coffee trees, sharing fifty-fifty the expense and profit of the enterprise. In 1855, as reported by two American missionaries, Kidder and Fletcher, there were about a thousand colonists, including children, on the Vergueiro estates,[15] and the system served as a model for other planters large and small.

The Emperor had always encouraged official immigration of laborers from Europe. Indeed as far back as the days of Dom João VI the crown had thought in terms of a colonization policy to prepare for transition from servile to free labor. In 1818 a surtax was imposed on imported Negroes, the proceeds to be used to establish colonies of European immigrants. But very little was accomplished, even though in 1819 German Swiss founded the town of Nova Friburgo, today a flourishing city in the state of Rio de Janeiro. Under the first Emperor several colonies were established in the southern provinces, notably the German settlement of São Leopoldo in Rio Grande do Sul in 1824, and Santo Amaro in São Paulo four years later. Some of the colonists were mercenary soldiers promised land by the government or disbanded after the great mutiny of 1828. Under the Regency a Colonization Society was organized in 1835 to assist recently arrived immigrants, and it ministered to several thousand newcomers. Up to 1850

[15] D. P. Kidder and J. C. Fletcher, *Brazil and the Brazilians, Portrayed in Historical and Descriptive Sketches* (Philadelphia, 1857), pp. 406–413.

some 19,000 colonists are said to have entered Brazil under official and private auspices.

When the supply of labor from Africa ceased with the suppression of the slave trade, European immigration tended for a while to increase, especially in the south where land was more available and slaves were fewer. And in 1857 seventeen colonies were reported, founded by the imperial government or by the provinces, although they were rarely as successful as those under private auspices. For a time in the 1860's the stream slackened because of reports abroad that contractual arrangements were not lived up to, resulting in disillusionment and ill-treatment. After the passage of the Law of Free Birth in 1871, and with the expansion of coffee planting in the interior, European immigration again increased, especially of Italians who were more adaptable perhaps to the Brazilian way of life than colonists from the north of Europe.

All in all, however, results were meager, partly because of official inertia, partly because the white free laborer was not attracted to a country where agricultural work was equated with human slavery. European immigration, in fact, was never an important element in the history of Brazil so long as the institution of chattel slavery survived. The majority of the planters clung to their old ways, either in the belief that slave labor was more advantageous, or because of the considerable capital they had invested in the Negro, sometimes representing their entire fortune. Only after abolition did immigration rise to many thousands yearly, and then the newcomers were mostly from southern and eastern Europe.

Under the impact of abolitionist propaganda, and inspired by the eloquence of Joaquim Nabuco, popular antislavery sentiment gained in intensity throughout the nation from north to south. Public meetings, articles in the daily press, and abolitionist societies deepened the ferment and wore down the reluctance of a Parliament dominated by slavery interests.

The question cut across conventional party interests and caused confusion in political alignments. Liberals were divided into hostile factions, as were the Conservatives, with resultant great ministerial instability. Both sides blamed the Emperor: the slave owners charged him with responsibility for the origin and progress of the abolition movement, the abolitionists for his failure to act with greater precipitation. Extremists in both camps indulged in the bitterest denunciations and in their fury attacked the institution of monarchy itself.

Since the acceptance of the Law of Free Birth, the gradual extinction of slavery in the course of nature was anticipated, perhaps by the end of the century. In the parliamentary struggle the question was whether its consummation should be hastened by legislative action; and at bottom was also the question of indemnification of the slave-owners, although it was rarely mentioned by either side. The simple fact of the matter was that abolition was bitterly opposed by the majority of the rural aristocracy, the class that possessed most of the great private fortunes and the paramount electoral influence throughout the nation. The party chiefs themselves were many of them large proprietors of slaves, or in any case their political prestige was contingent on the favor of this group. To show great sympathy for abolition would immediately alienate this indispensable support of the most powerful social and political estate in the country.

The Liberal governments in power since 1878 were finally forced to meet the issue at least half-way. Five Liberal cabinets had resisted the abolitionist pressure by direct opposition or compromise. In 1884 the Emperor, after consultation with the principal Liberal leaders, intervened to call to office a known abolitionist, Manoel de Sousa Dantas. His program included increase of the redemption fund, a new registration of all slaves and their release if unregistered, restriction of the transfer of slaves from one province to another, and the liberation of all slaves when they reached the age of sixty. When the Chamber rejected the measure, Dantas called for a dissolution, but as the ensuing election was indecisive, he resigned to be replaced by José Antônio Saraiva. The new cabinet succeeded in getting through the Chamber a law in general similar to Dantas' bill, whereupon to insure its acceptance by the Conservative Senate, Saraiva resigned and Dom Pedro called upon the president of the Senate, the Barão de Cotegipe, to form a Conservative ministry. The bill became law on September 28, 1885. It liberated all slaves when they reached the statutory age, but as freedmen they had to continue to serve their former masters for three years. Those already older had to be cared for by their former owners. The new law affected some 120,000 Negroes.

Still the abolitionists were not satisfied, although the operation of the Laws of 1871 and 1885, together with that of the emancipation funds, presaged the rapid disappearance of slavery without serious economic disturbance. The number of slaves had fallen since 1871 by more than half, to somewhere between 500,000 and 750,000. The situation became more and more critical. Many owners failed to register their slaves. Negroes were openly encouraged to flee from the plantations and were aided and protected in a kind of "underground railway" such as existed in our own South before 1860. Clergy denounced the slavery institution from the pulpit. Abolitionist lawyers defended the Negroes if captured, and magistrates found pretexts for releasing them. Voluntary liberation gained headway. In February 1887 the city of São Paulo celebrated the anniversary of its founding by liberating with funds raised by popular subscription all the slaves within the city. In 1886 and 1887 officers of the army protested against orders to pursue fugitive slaves and openly ranged themselves with the anti-slavery elements. Measures of the plantation owners to resist the wholesale abandonment of their lands raised the fear of servile revolt against the whites.

The final blow fell in May 1888 when the Emperor again was absent in Europe and his daughter and heiress-apparent, Dona Isabel, was ruling as regent. Dom Pedro had fallen seriously ill in February 1887 with diabetes — he was then 61 years old — and in June had sailed with the Empress to Europe for medical consultation and treatment. The Princess Regent, herself a confirmed abolitionist, was convinced that to hold out any longer was dangerous, that the government must keep pace with public sentiment even if it affected the stability of the monarchy. On the resignation of the unsympathetic Conservative cabinet of Cotegipe in March 1888, she summoned another Conservative, but an abolitionist, João Alfredo Corrêa de Oliveira from Pernambuco, to form a ministry. The new government, apparently at the Regent's bidding, introduced a bill on May 8 providing for the immediate extinction of all human slavery in Brazil with no provision for compensation to the owners. It passed both houses by overwhelming majorities and was signed by the Princess five days later. It extinguished property said to be worth over 300 million dollars.[16]

At the time Dom Pedro lay grievously ill in Milan. Had he been well and in Brazil, he doubtless would have exerted his influence to indemnify the planters. But the nation was engulfed in a wave of moral indignation that demanded immediate action and brooked no compromise. When the votes were taken in Parliament, crowds in the galleries shouted *viva's* and rained flowers upon the legislators. The press in general emphatically approved the measure, as did the people in all parts

[16] It is interesting to observe that in 1888, as in 1885 and 1871, the emancipation measures were put through by a Conservative ministry. As so often in English history, it was the Conservatives who ultimately achieved reforms advanced by the Liberals.

of the Empire. Eight days of festivities followed, torch-light processions, student demonstrations, bands of music. As Oliveira Lima remarked, the nation indulged in a delirium of enthusiasm such as Brazil had never seen or was ever to see again. Dom Pedro, who had contributed much to the education of public sentiment against slavery, recovered sufficiently to return to Brazil in August following the Emancipation Law, and was received with immense demonstrations of affection and loyalty. The emancipation, he declared, gave him the greatest happiness of his life.

The Conservative government of João Alfredo had thought in terms of later recompensing the slave owners, either by systematic appropriations in the national budget or by means of a foreign loan.[17] But no formula was found, and the abolitionists, on orders from the Minister of Finance of the later republican regime, Rui Barbosa, destroyed many of the official registers of slaves which were the only documents on which indemnification could be based. The imperial government, however, did establish a new agricultural bank which extended large credits to the landowners to offset the losses from emancipation.

The Golden Law — Lei aurea, as it was later called — "was scarcely more than the sanction of a preëxistent fact . . . the inevitable consequence of irresistible public opinion," [18] but it unavoidably occasioned great agricultural disorder. It affected not only the coffee-growing provinces of the south but also the more conservative, tropical, cotton-producing north — especially perhaps the north, where fewer private efforts had been made to meet the change halfway. Entire

[17] The government did contract a loan of £6,000,000 on the London market at 97 and 4½ per cent interest which was immediately covered. Liberato de Castro Carreira, História financeira e orçamentária do império do Brasil desde a sua fundação (Rio de Janeiro, 1889), p. 668. The total foreign debt of the imperial government at its fall in 1889 was £28,478,300.

[18] Calógeras, Formação histórica, p. 385.

families were completely impoverished. Most of the Negroes, as was to be expected, immediately abandoned the plantations for the hills or for the urban centers, but by no means all of them. Some remained as paid laborers on the estates or settled down in the old sugar and coffee areas on plots of land given them by the former masters or acquired on easy terms. The crops due to be gathered in May and September, however, were in great measure sacrificed. On the other hand, the old rural coffee aristocracy had been playing a losing game for years. Primitive methods of cultivation, soil exhaustion, and inefficient slave labor had undermined the solvency of most of the coffee viscounts and barons of the famous Paraíba valley. Abolition merely gave the *coup de grâce*.

Nevertheless, coffee was becoming, and remains today, the principal agricultural resource of the nation, its chief article of export to the world. And the sooner its production could be put on a more efficient, free-labor basis, the better for the continued prosperity of Brazil. In the coffee areas Negro slaves were rapidly replaced by Italian and other European immigrants who came to work the plantations on a coöperative basis. As has appeared, this immigration had long been encouraged in anticipation of abolition. But before 1888 these newcomers from Europe had never exceeded 30,000 a year. In 1889, 97,000 Italians entered Brazil, and 108,000 in 1891; and today the Italian element in the population of the key state of São Paulo equals in social and economic importance that of the Portuguese.

The abolition of the institution of slavery, involving the extinction of vast property rights, had for Brazil serious political and social consequences, as well as economic. The old Conservative Party had in the act signed its own death warrant. A considerable number of the electors passed over to the Liberals, others to the republicans, but the majority withdrew from the political arena, retired to their estates, or de-

parted for Europe.[19] By the same token, the prestige and
social influence of a class that represented the best elements of
the Empire were largely destroyed. Emancipation without
compensation also alienated from the monarchy the less progressive planters, perhaps the majority, provoked bitterness
and resentment among the landowners who had refused to
see the writing on the wall, and furnished a pretext for political disaffection. The bonds of common interest with the
crown had been broken. The planter aristocracy had been
one of the mainstays of the Empire. Its estrangement helped
to make possible the downfall of the monarchy in the following year.

[19] *Ibid.*, p. 386.

Chapter Six

EDUCATION — ELECTIONS —
THE CHURCH

Brazil had gained little from the Paraguayan War except prestige and the moral satisfactions of victory. Of material advantage there was none save the "rectification" of a frontier with Paraguay in the remote interior. The struggle left her with an immense foreign debt, a currency depreciated by large issues of paper money, and perennial deficits in public finance. Nevertheless, in spite of the economic regression caused by the war, the Empire in the 1870's continued to experience a slow but steady material expansion, reflected in the growth of international trade, an over-all stability of foreign exchange, and the improvement of communications through the extension of railway and telegraph lines. The milreis, fixed by law in 1846 at a parity of 27 pence, had suffered grievously during the war, but after the peace gradually recovered and, although subject to violent fluctuations, averaged about 25 pence.[1] Foreign commerce which in 1850 amounted to about 150,000 contos ($75,000,000), increased by nearly 300 per cent, chiefly because of the ascending exports of coffee. The renewed attraction of capital from

[1] Castro Carreira, *História financeira e orçamentária*, pp. 679–691.

Europe maintained a relative stability in the balance of international payments, and in spite of shifting monetary and tariff policies, and occasional economic setbacks, public finance and the credit of the Empire abroad were in general sound. The over-all economic situation, however, continued to be one of financial instability, sharp oscillations in the expansion and contraction of the circulating medium, and consequent effects upon production and speculative activities.

Only in the realm of public education the progress of Brazil under the Empire was singularly slow, although it was always a preoccupation of the Emperor. Primary education was the responsibility of the local, municipal authorities, secondary schools were few and confined to the larger cities, and the country remained without a university organization until sixty years later under the Republic. The legacy from colonial times had been very meager. The closing of the Jesuit colleges when the order was expelled in 1759 had dealt a heavy blow to secondary education. Until the end of the eighteenth century, there was very little elementary instruction except privately or in the monasteries. In contrast to the Spanish American communities, colonial Brazil possessed no higher professional faculties, or even a printing press. Parents who were able and so inclined sent their sons overseas to Portugal's major university at Coimbra or to other foreign institutions. Toward the end of the era, however, literary societies and learned "academies" appeared in some of the principal cities, and Brazil was producing its share of scholars and jurists who filled important political and academic posts in Portugal and provided the leaders of the new empire in America.

The ill-fated constituent assembly of 1823 drew up a law providing for two universities, one in São Paulo, the other in Olinda, of course never promulgated. Four years later Brazil's first national Parliament by law created a Law School in each of these two cities which have survived to the present day, and from whose halls have come most of the political leaders of the nation. Faculties of medicine existed in Rio de Janeiro and Bahia from the days of independence, and in 1826 a School of Fine Arts was organized in Rio. The Military Academy established by Dom João VI, which supplied both the civil and the military engineers, was in 1874 separated as an engineering school from the Ministry of War and transformed into a Polytechnical Institute. In 1877 the agricultural institute of São Bento das Lages was set up, largely through the Emperor's efforts. Otherwise no significant additions were made to professional education under Dom Pedro II. Elementary schools both public and private somewhat increased in number in the later decades of the Empire, principally in the major cities, but in the country at large educational facilities were appallingly inadequate, if they existed at all, and the vast majority of the population, perhaps 80 per cent, remained illiterate.

Of the public secondary schools the most important was the celebrated Colégio Dom Pedro II in Rio de Janeiro, created in 1837 by Bernardo de Vasconcelos. As its patron the Emperor maintained a deep interest in the school and visited it regularly and often. Indeed he was sharply conscious of the educational shortcomings of the nation. To the very end, in the annual Address from the Throne he urged upon Parliament the establishment of additional technical schools and of one or two national universities. By these and other public utterances, by his attendance upon and inspection of all kinds of schools high and low, and by his encouragement and patronage of talented young men, painters, poets, and musicians, often subsidizing them from his private funds, he assumed a genuine leadership in the nation. His personality is especially associated with the Instituto Histórico e Geográfico Brasileiro, the oldest surviving learned academy in Latin America, of which he was elected patron and protector at its first session in 1839, when he was only thirteen years of age. At its fortnightly meetings he was a familiar figure, and he helped in many ways, by suggestions and by gifts of prizes, books, and manuscripts, to stimulate its scholarly activities.

Not unrelated to the problem of illiteracy was that of the electoral processes under the Empire. National elections were almost never "free" in the sense that they were the genuine expression of a popular mandate, presuming that under the circumstances such a mandate was possible. Corrupt practices of every sort insured the victory of those in control of the local administration, and given the extreme centralization of authority under the Constitution, this meant control by the imperial ministry in Rio de Janeiro. National elections were indirect, in two stages. The voters chose electors, and these in turn selected the deputies to the Parliament. The system, although it had several times been amended and refined, including minority representation in 1875, gave room for all kinds of irregularities, interference by the police, by local magistrates and landowners, to secure the choice of a favorable electoral board. "The only moral fault of the party in power was to lose an election. And to that end any device however fraudulent was permissible." [2]

Closely allied with the electoral problem was that of the local judiciary, especially in the more remote parts of the country. Courts were often corrupt, the laws were not respected or enforced, and personal and property rights were ignored. Judicial tyranny and dishonest elections went hand in hand. And as elections were generally associated with resort to the Moderating Power as a means of bringing about a rotation of parties in the government, critics were apt to put all the blame on the monarchy. It was the "result" of the so-called "personal power" exercised by the Emperor, although Dom Pedro, increasingly conscious of the national shortcom-

[2] Calógeras, *Formação histórica*, p. 373.

ings, repeatedly urged judicial and electoral reform. The independence of the judiciary was assured by reforms as early as 1871, realized under Conservative auspices, and Dom Pedro took steps to see that they were meticulously enforced. But it was a problem that could not be solved by legislation alone.

Nor could electoral irregularities be cured by mere resort to legislation, although reform became one of the burning questions of the 1870's. Change waited rather upon the spread of education and of a civic conscience in the population at large. It became more and more the conviction, however, of many political leaders and of the Emperor himself that direct election and single electoral districts provided the solution. This was perhaps in part a reflection of a contemporary movement in European democracies to generalize the suffrage and reinforce popular government. It had long been included in the Liberal program, but as to the best means of achieving it, whether by constitutional amendment or by ordinary law, opinions differed. The Conservatives, firmly intrenched in power since 1868, were in no eager mood to change anything. Although Dom Pedro secured from their leaders a promise to support the reform, nevertheless to insure its enactment he dismissed the cabinet in 1878 and called the Liberals into the government. Three years elapsed, however, before legislation was achieved. Many feared that alteration of the Constitution might provide occasion for other changes advocated by radicals and republicans, such as abolition of the Moderating Power and the life Senate. Finally a ministry headed by Senator José Antônio Saraiva sponsoring reform by legislation gained the support of the Senate and the Conservatives. The new law, promulgated in January 1881, provided for direct elections and included detailed provisions governing the creation of electoral districts and the qualifications and registration of voters. In a general election under the new dispensation held later in the year while Saraiva was still President of the

Council the code was observed to the extent that two of his ministers were defeated by opposition candidates! But in succeeding years party interests overwhelmed public interest, and the old practices and official pressures returned Chambers almost unanimously for the party in control of the electoral machinery.

Thereafter Dom Pedro made less serious efforts to maintain his prerogatives, possibly because of declining physical strength, probably disillusioned of any hope that the dynasty would survive his lifetime. To escape the ambiguity in which he was placed, he more and more limited himself to ministries chosen in harmony with the sentiments of the existing Chamber, and designated senators in accordance with the cabinet's wishes. Yet the personal powers of the Emperor remained a constant refrain of the opposition, whether in Parliament or in the press. If a ministry fell, the President of the Council was the first to give currency to what he called the real reason for his resignation, i.e., the imperial will. Although the sovereign had occasionally imposed his point of view, the record shows that Dom Pedro, in his role of moderator between parties, was careful never to abuse his powers, that he generally displayed unusual discernment and discretion in his choice of upper-bracket personnel, whether ministers, senators, judges, or diplomats, and in his concern for administrative morality. It is well to remember, however, that most of the political leaders, both Conservatives and Liberals, were landowners or sons of landowners, i.e., were drawn from the same aristocratic class. The parliamentary regime therefore implied a close union between this aristocracy and the throne. The throne was likely to survive only so long as a good understanding between them continued, especially as in the rest of the Western Hemisphere monarchy was looked on as an anachronism. By the growing estrangement between the political parties and the crown, the social and political substructure on which the monarchy rested was seriously weakened. Some of the foundation stones were giving way. And when in 1889 a sudden crisis appeared, there remained in the nation neither the will nor the strength to resist it.

Another traditional buttress of monarchy in Brazil, as in the Old World, was the official Church, always a citadel of conservatism. This support too was weakened by a quarrel with the crown over Freemasonry and the imperial control of ecclesiastical administration. The Constitution of 1824 recognized an official religion, Roman Catholic and Apostolic; and the Papacy for its part accepted the *Padroado,* or right of ecclesiastical patronage inherited by the imperial crown from its Portuguese predecessor. As received from the Pope in the sixteenth century, this was primarily the right to nominate to church benefices, and to require royal permission for the publication within the kingdom of any communication from the Roman Curia. But through the medium of regalistic lawyers, especially in the eighteenth century, the prerogative had been vastly extended. Ministers of State ordered bishops to observe the canons of the Council of Trent in appointments to parishes; prohibited their leaving the diocese without permission of the government on pain of having the see declared vacant; controlled the establishment of churches and other religious foundations; forbade religious orders to receive novices; even approved a theological compendium for use in the seminaries. In short, the Church as a corporation had been transformed into a servant of the secular power as a department of state.

The Brazilian clergy by and large were very liberal, and appeared to accommodate themselves easily to this situation. Many of them were active in the Masonic Order. In the republican revolts in Pernambuco in 1817 and 1824, members of the clergy appeared prominently among the leaders. And they enjoyed generally a great prestige, played an important role in the political parties and in parliamentary debates of the first half of the century. The prelates were usually men of a high order morally and culturally. But as in colonial times most of the rank and file led rather scandalous lives. Clerical celibacy scarcely existed. Indeed the Minister of Justice, Aureliano de Sousa, in a letter to Fabbrini, the papal delegate, in 1834, declared that the government might abolish at its pleasure such matters of discipline as clerical celibacy, which, he said, "does not exist anyway." [3]

Diogo Antônio Feijó, a leader among the more radical clergy, had advocated the abolition of clerical celibacy as early as 1823.[4] When four years later such a proposal was submitted to the Chamber of Deputies, he emphatically supported it both in the House and outside; and the question was revived when he became Minister of Justice under the Regency in July 1831. In the following year the General Council of the Province of São Paulo, prodded by the central government, requested the bishop to abolish celibacy in his diocese — which gave occasion for an inquiry directed by the papal delegate to the Minister of Justice and the reply noted above. Also in June 1831 the Ecclesiastical Commission of the Chamber had proposed changes in the marriage laws, admitting divorce for adultery, and placing the jurisdiction in marital cases within the competence of the civil courts.[5] These questions soon became entangled in a controversy with the Papacy over confirmation of a bishop of Rio de Janeiro. In March 1833 the Regency nominated to the vacant see Antônio Maria de Moura, a professor in the Law Faculty of São Paulo and active in politics, who apparently had been identified with these radical proposals. Pope Gregory XVI refused confirmation until Moura formally cleared himself of such uncanonical per-

[3] J. Dornas Filho, *O Padroado e a igreja brasileira* (São Paulo, 1938), p. 70.
[4] Manoel Cardozo, "The Holy See and the Question of the Bishop-Elect of Rio, 1833–1839," *The Americas*, X, 17–18.
[5] *Ibid.*, p. 6.

suasions. The dispute continued into Feijó's term as Regent, and the government took a high hand, insisting on the Pope's acquiescence, and even threatening to break off relations with the Holy See.[6] In fact, Feijó has commonly been charged with envisaging a separate National Church, but this is doubtful.[7] With the change of Regent in 1837, came a reversal of attitude in Rio, and a new ministry expressed willingness to respect Rome's misgivings. Moura formally renounced his see in a letter to the Minister of Justice in October 1838, and in the following year Manoel do Monte Rodrigues de Araújo was presented by the government and duly preconized by Pope Gregory.

This dispute of 1833–1837 was the only serious crisis in relations between the Empire and the Church until the quarrel with the bishops in the 1870's. As for the educated laymen, it seems that religion did not weigh too heavily upon most of them. Portuguese Catholicism in general was "softer," more humane, less inflexible, less puritanical, than the Spanish variety. The Emperor, scrupulously educated as a Catholic, was in this as in everything tolerant, deferential — not personally a practicing Catholic although as Head of the State he participated in official religious ceremonies. He favored a law permitting civil marriage and welcomed Protestant missionaries to the country. Financial aid was given by the imperial treasury to German Protestant clergy in the southern provinces. Dom Pedro, however, was far from being a materialist. He corresponded with Ernest Renan and other liberals in Europe, and was familiar with their writings and those of the New England Unitarians. He had an especial admiration for Wil-

[6] *Ibid.*, pp. 27ff. In September 1835, three days before Feijó was chosen Regent, the ministry also nominated him to the vacant see of Mariana, but under the circumstances he filed the decree and it was never presented to Rome. He did not formally renounce the appointment, however, until 1838, when he also publicly retracted many of his earlier speeches and writings. *Ibid.*, 47, 65.

[7] Cf. above, Chapter III, note 3.

liam Ellery Channing. "I am religious," he wrote on one occasion, "because morality, which is a quality of intelligence, is the foundation of the religious idea." [8]

Convents and monasteries were numerous in Brazil. But the conventual life was not generally attractive to Brazilians, especially since the friars, with few exceptions, did not recommend themselves for their piety or other virtues. Many of the friars were foreigners. Yet the monastic orders were wealthy, especially the Benedictines, with estates and plantations bequeathed by those who sought thus to redeem their errors, estates as a rule badly managed. The history of the Empire abounds in conventual scandals, often financial, that required correction by the government, to the prejudice of religion. In an effort to arrest the decadence of the religious orders, initiated by Nabuco de Araújo, then Minister of Justice, in 1854, the government had the loyal coöperation of the episcopacy.[9]

Although the crown never succeeded in negotiating a formal concordat with Rome, the Holy See did not deliberately antagonize the imperial government. In fact, it even gave consent to mixed marriages in Brazil, requested in order to encourage Protestant immigration, a concession never granted to the nations of Spanish America. On the other hand, since the publication of the famous Syllabus of Pope Pius IX in 1864, ultramontane influences had spread among the secular clergy, many of whom, under the direction of several eminent and virtuous bishops, displayed a new spirit of discipline and moral earnestness.

The Syllabus claimed for the Church the control of all culture, of science, and of the whole educational system. It rejected liberty of conscience and of worship, and demanded complete independence of the Church from state control. In-

[8] Williams, *Dom Pedro the Magnanimous*, pp. 166–173.
[9] *Ibid.*, p. 173.

deed, ultramontanism, as revived in the nineteenth century, went a step farther and maintained that it was the duty of the state to carry out the wishes and instructions of the Papacy. To that extent the state was subordinated to the Church, a union of altar and throne in which the altar controlled the throne. And this doctrine was accentuated by the proclamation by an Ecumenical Council in 1870 of the Infallibility of the Pope. It was these circumstances that engendered the Kulturkampf in Germany in the 1870's and the emergence of the so-called "Old Catholic" opposition. A similar quarrel was to plague Brazil.

Until 1872 no serious religious conflict disturbed the peace of the country. The apple of discord was the incompatibility of the Papacy and Freemasonry, brought to a head by an encyclical of Pope Pius in 1864, to which the Syllabus had been attached, denouncing the Masonic Order. In Brazil it never received the requisite imperial sanction. Masonic lodges flourished in Brazil; they had played an important part in the independence movement. But the old revolutionary spirit in them had long ago disappeared. In no sense had they been antireligious or anti-Catholic, as in many parts of the Old World. Many of the clergy, as has been noted, were active in their ranks. In 1872 the President of the Council, Visconde de Rio Branco, was Grand Master in Brazil, as Dom Pedro I had been in his time.

The first incident occurred in Rio de Janeiro in March 1872. A priest, Father Almeida Martins, delivered an address at a meeting of the Grand Lodge called to commemorate the passage of the Law of Free Birth by the Rio Branco government the year before. His bishop ordered him to forswear Masonry on pain of suspension. Almeida failed to comply, and when the bishop hesitated to carry out his threat, Almeida defied his superior by celebrating a Mass ordered by a Masonic lodge. And the conflict was on.

The Masons retorted by bitter attacks in pamphlets and in the press against the clergy. The challenge was picked up by Bishop Vital María Gonçalves de Oliveira of Pernambuco, an ardent and devoted young Capuchin friar educated in France, recently consecrated, and imbued with ultramontane doctrines. When in June the Masons of Recife announced a Mass to celebrate the anniversary of the lodge's founding, Bishop Vital forbade his clergy to officiate at any Mass under Masonic auspices. Most of the clergy obeyed. But when the *irmandades*, religious brotherhoods largely composed of laymen, were ordered in December to expel their Masonic members as excommunicated persons, they refused. The bishop thereupon suspended the religious functions of the Brotherhood of the Santissimo Sacramento, and placed its chapel under an interdict. In a pastoral letter earlier in the year, he had denounced not only Freemasonry but the Padroado as well.[10]

The *irmandades* were a conspicuous feature of Brazilian society. Many possessed large endowments, and they directed almost all the institutions of social welfare: orphanages, hospitals, reformatories, schools for adults. Foremost were the brotherhoods of the Santa Casa de Misericórdia which existed in almost all the cities and enjoyed the special protection of the state. The largest and most famous hospital in Brazil was the Misericórdia of Rio de Janeiro, founded by the Jesuit José de Anchieta back in 1582, and open day and night to receive the sick and distressed of all races and religions.

The Brotherhood of the Santíssimo Sacramento appealed to the crown, and in June 1873, after long and scrupulous consideration by the Council of State presided over by the Emperor, the government ordered Bishop Vital to remove the interdict within a month. Meantime the bishop had written to the Pope,

[10] Dornas Filho, *O Padroado*, pp. 110ff. Dornas provides the best recent statement of the Question of the Bishops. Although he does not always clearly indicate his sources, he includes most of the official documents. The following pages are based frankly upon his account of the struggle.

who replied on May 29 recommending the suspension of the ecclesiastical censures for a year, but if worst came to worst, excommunication of the Masonic Order, dissolution of the rebellious brotherhoods, and organization of new ones. This brief, in defiance of the law, Bishop Vital published, and he not only refused to submit to the imperial order but suspended his dean (who happened also to be a Mason) because he accepted from the president of the province the post of director of one of the public schools. The result was a hostile street demonstration in which the Jesuit college was sacked and the machinery of two Catholic newspapers destroyed. Meantime the bishop was suspending from their religious functions other brotherhoods of Recife until by September 1873 all had been put under interdict except three. The government replied by directing the civil authorities to oblige the clergy to proceed with religious services despite the bishop, but had no success. It therefore on September 27 ordered legal action to be brought against Bishop Vital for violation of the Constitution and the Criminal Code.

Meanwhile there were public, and often sanguinary, disorders in the provinces, by Catholic fanatics on the one hand, by anti-Jesuit demonstrators on the other, incited by the public press for and against the bishop. In Parliament and in the highest social circles sentiment was divided. Among those supporting the government opinions varied as to the penalties that should be imposed. Some were for sequestering the "temporalities," i.e., revenues ecclesiastical and private; others counseled the expulsion of the bishop from the country as the contumacious official of a foreign power.[11] In December Bishop Vital was ordered brought to Rio for trial by the Supreme Court of Justice, and a fortnight later he was arrested under

---

[11] It is said that the government sent an emissary to the bishop urging him to take leave of absence until the incident had blown over, but he curtly refused.

protest in his palace in Recife and transported on a ship of war to the capital. On February 21, 1874, he was condemned to four years imprisonment at hard labor and costs. The Emperor shortly after commuted the sentence to simple imprisonment.

Bishop Vital had been joined in his crusade by the Bishop of Pará, Antônio de Macedo Costa, a Sulpician of notable but intolerant personality who was already in conflict with the Liberal Party in his own diocese. Three years older than Bishop Vital, and like him educated in France where Free-masonry had always been anticlerical, he never understood that its spirit and objectives in Brazil were the inverse of those in Europe. The battle began with the publication of a pastoral letter on March 25, 1873, ordering the brotherhoods to dis-sociate themselves completely from Freemasonry on pain of interdict. The results were similar to those in Pernambuco: appeal of the brotherhoods to the crown, deliberation by the Council of State, and orders in August to remove the interdicts within fifteen days; peremptory defiance by Bishop Macedo, and legal proceedings against him in November. Arriving in Rio de Janeiro in May 1874, on July 1 he received in the Supreme Court the same sentence as that meted out to Bishop Vital.

The conflict between the imperial government and the bishops in Brazil has been followed in some detail because it had important bearings upon concurrent procedures abroad at the Papal Curia. In August 1873 the government decided to appeal directly to the Holy See. Carvalho Moreira, Barão do Penedo, minister resident in London, was entrusted with a special mission to Rome to induce the Papacy to counsel peace and advise the bishops to conform to the Constitution and the laws. The mission seemed even to Penedo to be a hopeless one in view of the uncompromising position taken by Pope Pius and the Church since the publication of the Syllabus of 1864, especially as his instructions took the form virtually of an ultimatum. Penedo was informed that the government had ordered the trial of Bishop Vital, and was prepared if necessary to take even more energetic legal measures without awaiting the results of the mission. The government sought no favors, it only wanted justice, and would enter into no compromise. If questioned in these respects, the Ambassador was to state frankly what had been communicated to him.

Barão do Penedo, one of Brazil's most intelligent and accomplished diplomats, pursued a more circumspect course and found in the papal Secretary, Cardinal Antonelli, a friendly and understanding spirit. Pope Pius was apparently persuaded that, on the one hand, in sending to Bishop Vital the brief of May 29 he had been misinformed; and on the other, that his recommendation of mildness and restraint in the application of ecclesiastical censures the bishop in his exaggerated zeal had pointedly ignored. It appears that in conversation with Antonelli it was agreed that the Secretary in the Pope's name should write an admonishing letter in this sense to the bishop, to be delivered by the apostolic nuncio in Rio. Such a letter drawn up in Latin in December 1873 was read by Antonelli to the Ambassador, who hastened to inform his government of its purport: the Pope was pained by the actions of the bishop, who had misunderstood his letter of May 29; had he consulted with the Holy Father in season, the latter would have been spared this grief; the Pope had recommended moderation and clemency, but the bishop had persisted in the path of severity; the Pope therefore ordered him to restore things as they had been before the peace of the Church was disturbed.[12]

It appeared to be a complete diplomatic victory for the mission. However the Pope had earlier let it be understood that he expected the imperial government on its part to reciprocate by removing all the obstacles to the prompt restoration of

[12] Dornas Filho, *O Padroado*, p. 251.

peace. And Penedo had assured the Papacy of the conciliatory disposition of his government. News of the arrest of Bishop Vital, therefore, was a shock to both the Ambassador and the Pope. Penedo saw the whole structure of his diplomacy fall to the ground. He had been informed of the intentions of the government in his instructions, but was probably warranted in presuming that they would not be carried into effect. Pope Pius was justifiably indignant, and sent a message to the Emperor urging him to set the bishops at liberty. At the same time orders were dispatched to the nuncio in Rio to destroy the admonishing letter which already was in the hands of the imprisoned bishops. Its existence, however, had been divulged by the government, which now sought by negotiation in Rome to oblige the bishops to disclose the letter and fulfill its admonitions, under the circumstances a hopeless endeavor.

The Penedo mission and the suppressed papal letter gave opportunity for a vituperative and long-drawn-out campaign against the Ambassador and the government. Penedo was accused of having deceived the Pope as to the ultimate intentions of his superiors, or of having reported inaccurately the contents of a letter which he had not himself read. There is no doubt that the Papacy, in spite of the maladroitness of the imperial government in its instructions, had counted on the princely generosity of the Emperor to hold up any peremptory action against the bishops. The imprisoned bishops and their partisans denied that the letter had been written and accused the government of criminal levity in divulging a nonexisting document in order to humiliate them. By implication Penedo was an "unscrupulous inventor of apostolic letters." To many, the actions of the Roman Curia seemed ambiguous. It was not clear whether the Holy See supported the apostolic zeal of the bishops, or thought it preferable to spare the refractory brotherhoods. Echoes of the controversy have come down to our own time.

The arrest and imprisonment of the bishops was clearly a blunder, in its inception and its procedure. The prejudices of the Supreme Court were obvious. The Emperor himself was not in the least inclined to indulgence. He approved of the government's course throughout; indeed it is said that he made known his wishes to the judges of the Supreme Court. The bishops had defied the Constitution, flouted the imperial authority and the national dignity. Dom Pedro was by conviction and by tradition a regalist. The vehemence and intolerance of the bishops had made the question a personal matter in which the honor of the crown was also involved. And most of the members of the Council of State shared this regalistic attitude, regarding the insubordination of the bishops as a brazen attempt, inspired by a foreign government, to usurp powers that incontestably belonged to the sovereign authority.

The points of view of the two parties, Church and state, were irreconcilable from the outset, and it would have been better for the peace of the nation and the welfare of the monarchy had the imperial government been content with the administrative penalty of sequestering the temporalities of the bishoprics, as indeed had been suggested in the Council. At least the government had excellent justification for halting the prosecution when it received word from Barão do Penedo of the papal letter censuring the bishops and ordering the suspension of the interdicts. The severe punishment decreed against them, on the contrary, not only called forth the vigorous protest of the apostolic nuncio and a sharp reproof from Pope Pius addressed personally to the Emperor, but left the bishops confirmed in their obduracy. The interdicts remained, clergy hostile to the government were assigned to diocesan vacancies, and the nation was brought close to the verge of a religious war. In Pernambuco and Pará governors of the diocese appointed by the condemned bishops and recognized as such by the provincial authorities, when they refused to raise the interdicts, were in turn prosecuted and condemned. And as the imperial government refused to accept any others designated by the bishops, as the cathedral chapters ignored orders to appoint vicars general to administer the dioceses, and provincial presidents therefore hesitated to recognize parochial appointments, the consequence was ecclesiastical anarchy.

The only reasonable way out of the impasse was commutation of the prison sentences, even though it meant the retreat of the government. The Conservative ministry of Rio Branco, which had been in office since 1871, fell in June 1875, and the ministry that followed under the presidency of the Duque de Caxias, also a high-degree Mason, had the courage to face the issue. One of its first steps was to insist with the Emperor that the bishops be pardoned, and on September 17, 1875, the decree of amnesty was issued, against Dom Pedro's personal wishes. The Papacy responded promptly with an order to lift the interdicts and restore the *irmandades* to the *status quo ante*, although this action was accompanied by the customary condemnation of Freemasonry. And Cardinal Antonelli, to the embarrassment of the bishops, publicly transmitted to them a copy of the famous suppressed letter. Owing to the recalcitrance of Bishop Macedo, the penalties imposed on the brotherhoods of Pará were not revoked until 1880. On the other hand, the total exclusion of the Masons from the *irmandades* of Brazil was never carried into effect.

The crusading Bishop Vital retired to Europe, where he died of tuberculosis of the larynx in the following year in Paris. The bishop of Pará was later elevated to the dignity of archbishop primate of Bahia, and as such witnessed the fall of the monarchy and the proclamation of the Republic. But the bitter resentments occasioned by the religious dispute were slow in healing. Whatever the outcome, the monarchy was bound to suffer. The liberals attacked the Emperor because he gave way and pardoned the bishops. The clergy and the conservatives were scandalized by the arrest and humiliation of the churchmen. The republicans, certainly not pro-clerical, cheered from the sidelines any development that embarrassed the crown. The consequence was an accentuation of anti-monarchical opposition that drew support from the discontented on all sides. Insofar as the clergy felt alienated from the crown, one of the traditional props of monarchy had been seriously undermined.

Chapter Seven

* * * * * * * * * * * *

SEEDS OF DISAFFECTION — THE ARMY
AND THE REPUBLICANS

In the decade of the seventies, as a consequence of the quarrel between the crown and the Church, many of the clergy became alienated, or at least indifferent to the fate of the monarchy. In the following decade an equally serious problem arose in relations between the government and the army. And the Republican Party in both cases was quick to seize the occasion to sow discontent with the imperial regime.

The army has filled a conspicuous place in the political history of all the Latin American nations, although less so in Brazil than in the Spanish republics. The long struggle for independence between 1809 and 1825 left the embryo republics largely militarized. Military chieftains, thrown to the surface by the conflict, held political control of their respective provinces or districts, and after the war not only declined to retire in favor of the civil power, but were soon contending among themselves for political control of the nation and access to the public treasury that went with it. The intellectuals and the propertied class in congress assembled might draw up high-sounding democratic constitutions, but the generals held the keys to power. And the people at large, accustomed to despotic rule under the Spanish monarchy, easily acquiesced. For several generations in most of the republics nearly all the presidents were military men, dictators whose authority rested on an army, and who could be pried loose from the government only by force, by resort to revolution. Even after the middle of the century, when government in many of the republics gradually reverted to an oligarchy of civilian elements, good correspondence with the military was generally in the cards. And this situation still holds in some of the republics today.

In Brazil after independence the role of the army was far less in evidence, although Dom Pedro I made much of warlike exploits and the military career, eventually to his own undoing. It can be said, moreover, that the Brazilians were not a militarily-minded people, not as martial perhaps as their Spanish neighbors, although quite as courageous, quite as steady under fire. In the war of 1825–1828 against Argentina over the possession of what now is Uruguay the imperial government had great difficulty in recruiting soldiers, for service at home or abroad. Nor did Dom Pedro receive any aid from an unsympathetic Parliament in his desire to improve the situation of the armed forces. The Portuguese element that survived in the army doubtless helped to make it suspect among patriotic Brazilians. And so he resorted to experiment with a mercenary army recruited by agents in Ireland, Germany, and Switzerland. Not as a pretorian guard, Dom Pedro explained, but to provide his subjects with an example of the military virtues! For desire to rule as a constitutional monarch was not a mere figure of speech in Dom Pedro as it was in most Spanish American dictators. In his simplicity he really believed it, in spite of his temperamental inability to live up to it. However, amid the political confusion and uncertainties of the time the army became really the instrument on which the Emperor depended to withstand the unruliness of the press, the Parliament, and the clergy.[1]

The mercenaries, as it turned out, proved to be anything but a mirror of the military virtues. Many of them, it will be remembered, the riffraff of Europe, were utterly undisciplined, and after the serious mutiny of 1827 in Rio de Janeiro they were disbanded, the Germans among them being sent to join their compatriot colonists in Rio Grande do Sul. The Argentine war itself, a virtual defeat for Brazil, only increased Brazilian distaste for military adventure and widened the breach between the Emperor and his subjects. In the popular uprising in Rio in April 1831, which forced the Emperor's abdication, the garrison joined, whether in genuine sympathy with the aims of the populace or in sheer insubordination, is not entirely clear. In any case, the rank and file soon got out of hand, indulged in robbery and public disorders in the streets of Rio, and discredited the Revolution they had helped to success, until Diogo Feijó as Minister of Justice disbanded them and created a National Guard to restore public order.

During the decade of the Regency, that period of domestic discord, of local, separatist revolts and virtual political anarchy, the military were one of the worst elements of disorder, either suborned by the radicals or played upon by the personal ambitions of their officers. And in the end, as public tranquillity was restored, these afflictions only served to discredit militarism among the Brazilians as an instrument of government. This was felt by none more than by the second Emperor, and the ill-concealed disfavor of the army and the navy in circles about the throne proved in the end to be one of the reasons for the Empire's collapse. In the early years, in fact, legislation

[1] Oliveira Lima remarks that the only really military phase in the history of Brazil was the reign of the first Emperor.

touching the armed forces had been singularly lacking, and it was only by a decree of February 22, 1839, that the army received a relatively systematic organization.

After the pacification of Rio Grande do Sul in 1845, the army entered upon a period of comparative calm and regularity, to which the influence of Marshal Caxias contributed while he was a member of the government in the 1850's. In the campaign against the Argentine dictator Rosas in 1852 the Brazilian contribution was chiefly naval. It was the long war against Paraguay in 1865–1870 that first gave Brazil a professional army of any consequence. It also greatly increased the army's feeling of self-importance, without inculcating a corresponding conviction of self-discipline. At the war's close the government seems to have felt some concern over an exaggerated prominence given to the military. On the return of the victorious regiments, it contrived to divest them of unnecessary display by playing down the music and the flags, and breaking up the military units, so much so that the Conde d'Eu, commander in chief and the Emperor's son-in-law, protested and threatened to resign.[2]

It also happened that 1870 was the year in which a Republican Party was for the first time formally organized, and in its quest for members it addressed itself to the armed forces. Whether, as is often said, the presence of Brazilian troops for so many years in the republics of the Río de la Plata, even though these countries generally suffered from dictatorship and revolution, exerted an influence on the political opinions of returning military officers, seems very doubtful. In any case, after the war there was renewed military restlessness, when officers were limited to dull, commonplace life in barracks in contrast to their former activity and wartime importance. Moreover, in imperial Brazil there was strangely lacking a correct military tradition that would keep the army in its

[2] Oliveira Lima, *O Império brasileiro, 1822–1889*, p. 146.

proper place in the state, divorced from political action. Army and navy officers were eligible to political office even while they were in active service. As members of Parliament they could criticize or attack with impunity the administration of their chiefs in the ministry, protected by their parliamentary immunity.

The methods of recruitment were in part responsible for the army's shortcomings. There was no obligatory military service; enlistment was effective only among the lower classes. In both army and navy the rank and file were Negroes, *mestizos*, and poor whites from the rural areas, many of them vagabonds or convicted of crime — men not lacking in courage or physical endurance, but crassly ignorant and illiterate, and pliant material in the hands of ambitious military schemers. This condition was not peculiar to Brazil. It was characteristic of the armed forces in all the Latin American countries, given the extreme poverty and illiteracy of the masses of the nations, and helps to account for the political instability in many of them. As one Brazilian wrote, "The officers were to them merely gold-braided foremen, who could order them whipped, who commanded them in assaults on the enemy, and whom with equal impudence they obeyed when they were told to assault civic positions."

The Emperor, with an intellectual's distaste for things military, did little to withstand the indiscipline of the army. Rather by his neglect he in a sense came to terms with it. That he was quite unsympathetic, as is sometimes said, is scarcely true, as had been attested by his intense and exhausting labors in the army's behalf during the Paraguayan War. But as Calógeras has remarked, Dom Pedro never completely comprehended its political and social significance in the organization of the modern state, especially in Brazil where the fusing of its disparate elements into a national unity was far from complete. What interest Dom Pedro displayed was more in the navy, which in all Latin American countries has been traditionally the more aristocratic arm.

Official indifference, or even deep distrust, was unfortunately shared by the two monarchical parties, and in consequence the technical requirements of the army and navy submitted to the government were frequently deferred or forgotten. Recrimination, growing estrangement between military and civilians, and increasing solidarity and *esprit de corps* among the officers, were perhaps the inevitable outcome. The ranking officer in the army was the Duque de Caxias, who was twice premier and who was genuinely loyal to the throne. And he used his powerful influence and his immense personal prestige to keep subversion and dissatisfaction in check. But after his death in 1880 there was increasing degeneration in morale and discipline. Colonels and generals in command of the provincial military districts participated in local politics, agitated their grievances in the press, aired their private quarrels in public, and carried their disputes into Parliament itself. High-ranking officers, deprived of the opportunity for glory and prestige in warfare, were tempted to seek compensation in a political career. The military question was complicated by the stand that many officers took in the abolition movement, and also by the fact that not only the republicans but the two monarchical parties, Conservatives and Liberals, sought confederates among the officers.

In the government of Dom Pedro II the Minister of War was generally, although not always, a civilian. And when attempts were made to separate officers from politics, they only served to widen the breach between the military and the administration. In 1884 regulations were issued that forbade public statements, written or oral, concerning the civil government by army and navy officers. Every article or speech had

to be sent to the Minister of War for preliminary approval.
The result was a series of military crises between 1884 and
1889.

This "military question" of proper relations between the
military and the civil power apparently first came into the
open in 1883, when a senator introduced a measure for the
creation of a *montepio* or insurance fund for military officers
with obligatory contributions. There was immediate opposition, an officers' committee was formed to that end, and a
lieutenant colonel, Sena Madureira, was selected to state in
the press its point of view. Thereafter every officer arrested or
censured felt it his right to air his case in public, and it was
this that occasioned the regulations issued by the Minister
of War in the following year. But in the beginning, perhaps
throughout, the conflict per se apparently had no political
character. Among the officers, as among civilians, were Liberals, Conservatives, and a few republicans. It reflected rather
a class solidarity, a tribal spirit that reacted against rules that
it deemed prejudicial or offensive, whatever party was in
power.

In 1886 a Lieutenant Colonel Cunha Matos requested an
investigation of one of his subordinates, a captain in his regi-
ment suspected of malversation of funds for military supplies.
It led to a polemic between one of the deputies in the Chamber
and Cunha Matos, in which the latter in signed articles in
the press took occasion to criticize the Minister of War. The
Minister censured him in an Order of the Day and put him
under preventive arrest for forty-eight hours, an action justi-
fied by military tradition. But this did not prevent a senator
and marshal of the army, Corrêa da Câmara, Visconde de
Pelotas, from defending his comrade-in-arms in the Senate.
He declared the light punishment inflicted to be an insult to
the whole army, and pleaded "military honor," which he
placed over every other consideration, even the laws of the

country.[3] It should be added, perhaps, that the Conservative ministry of the Barão de Cotegipe was then in office, and that Pelotas, a courageous cavalry officer of "impetuous arrogance" but little parliamentary discretion, was the military mouthpiece of the Liberal opposition.

Another incident in the same year had more far-reaching repercussions. The Lieutenant Colonel Sena Madureira, referred to above, who was an abolitionist and of republican persuasion, contributed articles on military affairs to a republican newspaper of Pôrto Alegre where he was stationed. In one of them he referred to a speech in the Senate in which he had been attacked for his abolitionist propaganda. Receiving a reprimand from the Minister of War, he publicly demanded a court martial to prove its injustice. The Minister refused it as *ultra vires*. Sena Madureira's colleagues in Pôrto Alegre drew up and signed a protest to the government against the decision of the Minister, and they were openly supported by the commandant of that southern military district, Marshal Deodoro da Fonseca, who was also vice-president in charge of Rio Grande do Sul. In the Senate Marshal Pelotas again led the assault against the cabinet.

Marshal Deodoro was a member of a distinguished military family and a veteran of the Paraguayan War; loyal, courageous to a degree, impulsive, very popular with the army, but without great political discretion; a Conservative and a monarchist. But in this case, for special reasons, he sided with his fellow officers against a Conservative Minister of War, and the news made a tremendous impression throughout the army. In correspondence between the Minister and Deodoro, the latter stanchly upheld the action of his officers. The government

[3] Curiously enough, this same marshal in a speech some months before had observed that Brazil did not possess an army, and that what it had under that name was utterly without discipline, citing the fact that of the 13,000 in the army, over half were incarcerated, including fifty-four officers. F. J. Oliveira Vianna, *O Occaso do império*, pp. 146–147.

therefore in December 1886 transferred him from his southern command to the important post of Quartermaster General. On his arrival in Rio de Janeiro, the military cadets received him in triumph at the dock. And Deodoro, now the focus of military discontent, was foolish enough to head a movement of opposition to the government to the point of calling for a public meeting of some two hundred army and navy officers in one of the city's theaters. There they voted, without discussion(!), that the open breach between the armed forces and the government could not be healed so long as the "unconstitutional" censures of the Minister of War continued, and they called upon the ministry to repair its error. Deodoro was empowered to communicate with the Emperor, and he wrote two letters asking for justice for the military.

The cabinet in its dilemma had earlier submitted the question to the Supreme Military Council for an opinion. The Council sustained the military thesis that officers, like all other citizens, possessed freedom of discussion in the press, except regarding differences within the services between officers, which if publicly debated would be subversive of discipline. In the face of these rebuffs the government beat a retreat, and the unhappy Minister of War, unsupported by cabinet or Emperor, resigned. The malcontents then went a step further, and Deodoro and the Visconde de Pelotas published a manifesto demanding the recall of the censures against the two officers. The Senate, hoping to dispose of the question once and for all by a complete submission, voted to advise the government virtually to cancel all notes involving disciplinary sanctions. The ministry, fearing further disorders, yielded, but the abject surrender was without effect. In fact, by this decision military officers were really invited to enter the political arena, and agitators, especially republicans, who constituted themselves the special advocates of the prestige of the armed services, were given free rein.

This was in 1887, and thereafter there was increasing rebelliousness among the officers and indiscipline in the rank and file: riots in the streets, conflicts with the police, and subversive propaganda in the radical daily press. And successive cabinets in 1888 and 1889 were unable, or afraid, to make headway against it.

There had always been some republicans in imperial Brazil; indeed even earlier, ever since the example set by the thirteen English colonies in North America. As far back as 1789 the famous conspiracy of the *Inconfidência* in Minas Gerais had republican connotations. A group of intellectuals — military officers, poets, and priests — united in a plot to put an end to local tyranny and strike for independence, frankly after the pattern of the United States. The leader was a young lieutenant, Joaquim José da Silva Xavier, because of his casual vocation as a dentist best known as "Tiradentes," or tooth-puller. The somewhat vague, unrealistic plot was betrayed to the authorities. Tiradentes was executed, drawn and quartered, and the other participants were exiled to Africa. The episode, however, left an aftermath of republican sentiment in Minas Gerais with which the monarchist movement for independence had to contend in 1821–22. The idealism and enthusiasm of the young republican martyr, and his serenity and self-effacement under trial, made him one of the national heroes of Brazilian history, especially after the victory of the republican movement exactly one hundred years later.

After the flight of the monarchy to Brazil, the revolts in Pernambuco against Dom João VI in 1817 and against Dom Pedro I in 1824 took an antimonarchical, republican slant. And during the Regency, as we have seen, republicanism ran riot, especially in the peripheral provinces, Rio Grande in the south and Pará in the extreme north. During the decade 1850–1860, an era of internal peace and increasing material pros-

perity and of success in war and diplomacy, republicanism was
quiescent. But it reappeared in the following decade and was
stimulated by the ministerial crisis of 1868. Two years later,
in November 1870, a Republican Club was organized in Rio
de Janeiro, which began publication of a journal and in December issued a Manifesto regarded as the official beginning
of the Republican Party.[4] To a degree it represented the more
radical, ultra-democratic wing of the Liberal Party inflamed
against the monarchy by the events of 1868. But it also, perhaps, was in some measure a reflection of events in France: the
overthrow of Napoleon III and the establishment of the Third
Republic. And always it was identified with the yearning for
federalism.

The party remained small, without an official representation
in the Chamber until 1884, when Prudente de Morais Barros
and Manoel Ferraz de Campos Sales were elected deputies
from São Paulo (later to become the first two civilian presidents of the Republic). It was strongest in the southern provinces, Rio de Janeiro, São Paulo, Minas Gerais, and Rio
Grande do Sul. There it had an active press and numerous
cells or "clubs" in the principal towns. Only in São Paulo,
however, did the movement have from the beginning a centralized organization and rigid party discipline, so that by 1889,
largely as a result of its skillful, opportunist tactics, it counted
nearly a fourth of the electorate.[5] The republicans were to be
found mostly in the larger cities and among students and
professional men. In the north, even in Bahia and Pernambuco,
intellectual centers where the abolitionist movement displayed
such intensity, republicanism seems to have found little foot-
hold. The majority of the socially and politically important
part of the nation, even if disillusioned with respect to the

---

[4] G. C. A. Boehrer, *Da Monarquia à república* . . . *1870–1889* (Rio de
Janeiro, 1954), pp. 31ff.
　[5] *Ibid.*, 118–119.

monarchy, showed little confidence in the republican system, as appeared from its lack of support in local and national elections. Nor is this remarkable given the example of the system as it operated in many of Brazil's neighboring states. It was only the economic distemper occasioned by abolition in 1888 that caused many to cross into the republican camp, trusting that a radical change in the form of government would redress their ills. And sensing this, the republicans stepped up their campaign.

The Republican Party from its inception in the Manifesto of 1870 demanded many of the changes advanced by the Liberals — electoral reform, federal decentralization, an elected Senate, abolition of chattel slavery — changes many of them that the Liberals seemed too divided or distracted to carry out. Some historians represent the Republican Party as having no concrete official program of its own, of adding nothing to the liberal currents of the time, indeed of even declining officially and openly to espouse abolition until very late (1887) in the hope of winning adherents among the rural aristocracy. Its one concrete objective was to abolish the monarchy, set up a government like that of the United States, and thereby like that country become rich and powerful. In any case, monarchy was out of date in the New World, and Brazil must set its course anew. But whether the democratic, republican ideal could be accomplished or not, whether it was adaptable to conditions in the nation, was not seriously pondered. A healthy tradition of local self-government essential in a federal republican regime scarcely existed, and the illiterate masses, especially in the rural areas, accustomed to the autocratic rule of the local territorial magnate or the provincial president, had little concept of abstract political principles or forms of government.

There can be little doubt, on the other hand, that the spread of republican ideas reflected to some degree a gradual change in the make-up of Brazilian society, a decline in relative importance and influence of the conservative agrarian class, and a corresponding increase in importance of the industrial and commercial elements of the cities who were generally more progressive, more open to new ideas. It is not without significance that in the later years of Dom Pedro's reign a considerable number of the barons and viscounts created by the Emperor were successful businessmen.

Dom Pedro, although conscious of these social changes, seemed quite indifferent to their implications for the survival of the dynasty. Apparently he believed that a republic was the ideal form of government. He implied as much in a note written in exile in 1891: he had only wished to contribute to a social situation in which a republic could be "planted," so to speak, by him himself. But as Emperor he felt that so long as the mass of his subjects were so largely illiterate and without preparation for democratic government, they were not ready for republican rule. Constitutional monarchy as set up in Brazil, with its Moderating Power, was a necessary transitional stage. On the other hand, he never thought of imposing it on the nation against the weight of public opinion. He not only tolerated, he seemed to encourage, the growth of republican sentiment. As Miss Williams tells us,[6] Dom Pedro on a visit to a school in São Paulo heard the teacher in a class advocating republican principles, and merely remarked on leaving that if Brazil became a republic he wanted to be its first president. He even chose as mathematics tutor for two grandchildren a well-known and zealous republican, Benjamin Constant Botelho de Magalhães. When Benjamin Constant raised with Dom Pedro the obstacle of his republican views, the Emperor replied, "That won't hurt — you may be able to convert them."[7]

[6] Williams, *Dom Pedro the Magnanimous*, p. 295.
[7] *Ibid.*, pp. 295–296.

Benjamin Constant was a popular professor in the Military Academy in Rio de Janeiro, and his influence in inculcating republican doctrines with the younger generation of officers was very great. Among other outstanding leaders in the attack on the monarchy, besides Morais Barros and Campos Sales already mentioned, were Quintino Bocaiuva, editor of the influential newspaper, *O Paiz*, founded in 1884; Antônio da Silva Jardim who in the late 1880's became the demagogic leader of a minority calling for revolutionary action; Aristides Lobo, one of the intellectual powers in the movement; and a brilliant young lawyer and journalist, Rui Barbosa. Bocaiuva, whose great influence was always exerted on the side of moderation, of evolution rather than revolution, became Minister of Foreign Affairs in the Provisional Government that followed the overthrow of the Empire, and Rui Barbosa Minister of Finance. Rui Barbosa, more ardently federalist than antimonarchical, was to be the standard-bearer of enlightened liberalism later under the Republic, and one of the most distinguished statesmen and international lawyers that Brazil has produced.[8]

Benjamin Constant was also one of the leaders in the spread of Positivist philosophy in the Empire, a phenomenon with which the coming of the Republic was closely associated. The writings of Auguste Comte made in the nineteenth century a profound impact upon intellectuals in all the countries of Latin America. They adumbrated the concept that true knowledge, and the progress of civilized society, are based exclusively on the methods and discoveries of the physical or "positive" sciences, denying therefore metaphysical speculation or ultimate causes or origins. As a political system Positivism was inimical to notions of monarchy, hereditary right,

[8] When the King and Queen of Belgium visited Brazil in 1922, they asked especially to meet Rui Barbosa. Since he was living in the country and because of age and infirmities was unable to come to Rio, they made a special excursion to pay their respects to him.

aristocracy. Yet as a matter of fact, its adepts showed little immediate concern for such considerations as democracy, equality, popular majorities, or the lot of the common man. Comte's ideal was a dictatorial republic, ruled by an elite. The watchwords of Positivist society were "Order and Progress." It was a philosophy that appeared as a godsend to the political and social oligarchies ruling everywhere in Latin America. It had also, especially in Brazil, its religious aspects. For revealed religion it substituted a religion of humanity, with a ritual and ecclesiastical organization of its own. A Postivist Church apparently still survives in Rio de Janeiro, with a small "ethical culture" following.

This Positivist credo, which excluded any purely traditional or metaphysical concept such as a personal monarch or sovereign, spread rapidly among the younger army officers. It even engendered, it is said, a feeling of disdain for wrangling civilian politicians and parties who were without benefit of the Comtist philosophy. To the army, perhaps, should be delegated the task of moral and political regeneration. But outside the Military Academy and the Polytechnic Institute, the number of its adherents was always very limited. Oliveira Lima has called Positivism the "Gospel of the Military Academy." Younger lieutenants and captains, he continues with some humorous exaggeration, knew by heart Auguste Comte rather than the classical military manuals of Jomini and Von der Goltz, and in their clubs discussed politics and literature rather than mathematics and ballistics. Positivism, however, exerted an important influence on the advent and organization of the regime that followed the Empire, owing to the circumstance that several conspicuous leaders of the Revolution were among its adepts. They became the counselors of the new government, playing a role somewhat like that of the famous *Científicos* grouped around the Mexican dictator, Porfirio Díaz, and the names of some of them later fill pages in the history of the Republic. The motto on the green and yellow flag of the Brazilian Republic today is "Order and Progress," the maxim of the Positivists.

Such was the general situation in the last years of the Empire: insubordination in the army, and rising antimonarchical, republican sentiment among military officers and in professional circles, including a few clairvoyant or discontented landowners. The crown was blamed for all the shortcomings of government, most of which grew out of the inexperience or lack of self-discipline of the nation itself. Meantime Dom Pedro was aging and in ill-health, although he was only sixty-three when he was deposed in 1889. Especially after the attack of diabetes in 1887, his mental activity and capacity for work seem to have declined. He appeared more detached from current happenings, less aware of the political developments that were undermining the Empire, more and more engrossed in his books and in his intellectual interests rather than in affairs of state.

And so there was a repetition of military "incidents," to the embarrassment or overturn of successive cabinets. In March 1888 a retired naval officer involved in a fracas with the police was arrested and put in the lockup. The Naval Club met and demanded the dismissal of the chief of police. The Conservative premier, Cotegipe, demurred, but finding the Princess Regent sympathetic with the Naval Club, the ministry resigned. The new government, also Conservative under João Alfredo, faced a similar crisis, this time in the city of São Paulo. It seems that the chief of police in the course of his normal duties and in connection with an encounter between the police and some soldiers, had entered the barracks of the 17th Battalion, but without first resort to all the requisite formalities. The officers chose to interpret this as disrespect, an affront to the dignity of the army, and the resultant outcry obliged the cabinet to dismiss the chief of police and remove the battalion to Rio. And both cases were exploited by the Liberal opposition, and especially by the republicans, to embarrass the government.

The last ministry of the Empire was a Liberal one, under the presidency of the Visconde de Ouro Preto. On the resignation of the cabinet of João Alfredo for lack of a working majority in the Chamber, the Emperor and his advisers endeavored to replace it with another Conservative government as most likely to preserve the nation from disintegration. But they were unable to find a Conservative statesman who could command a parliamentary majority; so Dom Pedro turned to the Liberals, and in June 1889 Ouro Preto agreed to organize a ministry.

Ouro Preto, lawyer and experienced politician, faced an almost impossible situation, a country seemingly preparing for a republic, the aristocracy disaffected or openly hostile, and in Parliament a minority antagonistic to the existing dynasty. That he was the most appropriate choice by the crown in the circumstances has been questioned. A forceful individuality, bold, courageous, of singular uprightness of purpose and immense personal pride, he lacked the tact and discretion, the gift of conciliation and compromise, that the crisis called for. Frank, imperious, inflexible, his conduct at times served rather as an aggravating factor in the struggle with the militarists. In an endeavor to combat republican propaganda and save the monarchy, "make the republic unnecessary," he immediately outlined a sweeping program of reforms, political, social and economic: enlargement of the suffrage, abolition of life-tenure for senators, greater autonomy for the provinces and municipalities, entire freedom of public meeting and of religion, financial aid to the landowners in the form of long-term low-interest loans, and liberalization of the laws touching banking and corporations. The program, however, did not contemplate complete federalization in the sense of the abolition or transfer of the Moderating Power exercised by the Emperor. To conciliate the military, the Ministries of War and Navy were entrusted to professional officers instead of to civilians as in the past. An admiral, Barão de Ladário, became Minister of Marine, and an adjutant-general, the Visconde de Maracajú, received the portfolio of War, although neither was a member of Parliament.

There was an immediate vote of lack of confidence by the Chamber, followed by dissolution and a general election. The election as usual resulted in a complete victory for the ministry. Only one republican and four or five Conservatives secured seats. Clearly it was by devious methods controlled by the central and local authorities, although in this instance perhaps necessary in order to secure a Parliament that would put through the extensive program that alone might save the monarchy. But the Liberals had temporized too long, too long displayed a fatal lack of courage and resolution, too long been torn apart by internal rivalries and dissensions. When the moment for decision came, it was too late. The new Parliament never met. A military *coup d'état* in November 1889 overthrew the monarchy and set up a Republic.

Chapter Eight

* * * * * * * * * * *

THE MONARCHY REPUDIATED

The collapse of the Brazilian Empire in 1889 resulted from a conjuncture of diverse circumstances: (1) the abandonment of the agricultural interest through the emancipation of the slaves without indemnification for the slave owners; (2) disregard by the throne of the privileges and immunities claimed by the state religion, the Roman Catholic Church; (3) the scarcely restrained insubordination and the class pride amounting almost to delirium of the armed forces; (4) subversive propaganda of the republicans, reinforced by the sectarian philosophical spirit of the Positivists.

But there were other circumstances that helped to account for the repudiation of the monarchy. One was the lack of a sense of responsibility in the monarchical parties themselves, both of which, ever since the ministerial crisis of 1868 and whenever the Emperor's exercise of the Moderating Power frustrated their partisan or personalist ambitions, indulged in bitter attacks on the Empire and the dynasty. Moreover, as happens in the case of the Communists in Brazil today, the major parties often made temporary alliances with the republicans in order to achieve immediate partisan ends, and tolerated the expression of republican sentiments within their own ranks.

Another misfortune was the unpopularity of the Princess Isabel and her husband, the Conde d'Eu, grandson of Louis Philippe of France.[1] Dom Pedro had two sons, but both had died in infancy. His elder daughter, Isabel Cristina, was therefore heiress to the throne. The Princess Imperial was a gracious lady, intelligent, able, extremely conscientious, and she had been carefully prepared by her father for the responsibilities of rule. But by many Brazilians she was believed to have marked absolutist and pro-clerical tendencies. In the quarrel between Church and state in the 1870's she had shown considerable sympathy for the bishops. As Regent she had opposed a bill of the religious liberals permitting Protestants to give their meeting-places the outward semblance of churches. The slave owners blamed her as Regent in 1888 for abolition without indemnification. In short, she was thought to lack the tolerance, the political detachment, of her father. These things militated against her popularity with many and alienated the increasing liberal sentiment throughout the country.

The Conde d'Eu had never been popular, in part doubtless because he was a foreigner. Of high character and intelligence, he was by nature rather dry, aloof, undemonstrative, with a French provincial's economizing instincts. A man of simple manners, home-loving, careless of his attire, shunning the parades and other public celebrations that appealed to the more emotional and prodigal Brazilians, he never commanded the sympathy or understanding of high political and social circles, or even perhaps of his father-in-law, the Emperor. Yet he was active in all good works, whether of charity or of public improvement. As Commander in Chief of the Allied armies during the later stages of the Paraguayan War, he served with distinction, and he never lost his interest in his former com-

[1] Dom Pedro's two daughters were married in the same year, 1864; the younger, Leopoldina Teresa, to Louis Augustus, Duke of Saxe-Coburg Gotha.

panions at arms, or in the organization and equipment of the military establishment. He was devoted to his adopted Brazil, but unhappily he never succeeded in winning the affection and the confidence of its people.

The Prince Consort was also believed to meddle in affairs of state, and to influence his wife in political matters. This influence, although grossly and maliciously exaggerated, was natural if not inevitable under the circumstances, but in a foreigner it was intolerable. The Prince never had a good press. As time went on, chauvinist suspicions and criticism increased, and republican and other hostile propaganda made the most of it. In spite of these handicaps, in the middle of 1889 he was sent by the government on a tour of the provinces to rekindle popular sentiment in favor of the monarchy. In São Paulo he was scurrilously attacked by the republicans, and by Rui Barbosa in the pages of his *Diário de Notícias*. On a visit to the northern provinces as far as Amazonas, he was apparently somewhat more courteously received, but under the circumstances the stratagem was rather ingenuous at best. In his excursion to the north, he was followed step by step by Antônio de Silva Jardim, one of the most violent of the republicans, to frustrate whatever good his efforts might accomplish.

Many Brazilians, therefore, seriously doubted that there would ever be a third reign of the Braganza dynasty. The aging Emperor was personally as much liked and respected as ever, and most of the republicans tacitly agreed to await the death of Dom Pedro before attempting any radical change. But as the Conservative statesman, Cotegipe, remarked, "The Emperor is the Empire, or (conversely) the Empire is the Emperor," meaning that the presence of Dom Pedro was the only obstacle to the proclamation of a new political order. And, as has been noted, the Emperor was failing rapidly in health. It was observed that when he delivered the Address from the Throne at the opening of Parliament on May 1,

1889, he was obviously feeble, walked with unsteady step, and did not read as well as usual. And this gave excuse for the introduction in the Chamber a fortnight later of an unfriendly resolution calling for a committee to examine whether he was still competent to rule. There is no doubt that for one reason or another he was less closely in touch with current developments that deeply concerned him and his family.

The "dynamic" of the military revolution of November 1889, as someone has said, was "military honor," the "prestige" of the army. Marshal Pelotas had declared in the Senate that the honor of the soldier was above every other consideration, and must receive satisfaction even if contrary to law. A circumstance early in the year contributed to the general disquiet. Because of a critical boundary dispute between Bolivia and Paraguay, which was to result in the sanguinary Chaco War forty years later, the Brazilian government sent a body of troops including two corps of the Rio garrison under command of Marshal Deodoro, out to Mato Grosso on the borders of Bolivia as an army of observation. This was interpreted by the military as part of a plan of the Conservative ministry of João Alfredo to weaken the army by distributing the units to the provinces, away from the capital. And although Deodoro and his sullen troops were recalled within a few months, the irritating effect remained. Even at the headquarters in Corumbá it had been asserted that the column would have its accounts to settle with the government on its return.

Possibly under the Liberal ministry of Ouro Preto that followed in June, such a plan was contemplated.[2] Several moves of the government seemed to lend credence to the belief. In the city of Ouro Preto, capital of Minas Gerais, as a result of

[2] Ouro Preto later flatly denied that he had any such intention, and declared that the only transference he made, of the 22nd Battalion to Amazonas, was on the advice of the Adjutant General, Marshal Floriano Peixoto.

bloody street riots provoked by the garrison, a violent conflict arose between the chief of police and the commandant; and the ministry, instead of dismissing the chief of police as demanded, ordered the 23rd Infantry to Ouro Preto to restore public order — the army to discipline the army! Later, because of disorders in Manaus, capital of the province of Amazonas far up the Amazon River, the government prepared to send the 22nd Infantry there. Moreover, the President of the Council had apparently entertained the idea of building up a more effective National Guard or militia as a counterpoise to a recalcitrant professional army. Exploited by the political opposition, the plan only served, as might be expected, as an added irritant to the military class. At any rate, stiffening of resistance by the Ouro Preto ministry convinced army officers that it was deliberately hostile to them. Marshal Deodoro appealed by letter to the Emperor against the ministry's policies, but received no reply. To the military mind there seemed to be but one remaining solution, removal of the ministry by direct action.

The Emperor, meantime, remained strangely oblivious of the implications of the situation. When in late October, on the occasion of a visit to Rio of a Chilean cruiser, a banquet was tendered to its officers at the Military Academy, Benjamin Constant in an address of greeting bitterly attacked the government for its treatment of the army, before the visitors and the acting Minister of War. Ouro Preto, highly incensed, rebuked the Minister for failing to protest, dismissed the Commandant of the Academy, and prepared to punish the culprit himself. But Dom Pedro intervened: "Benjamin is an excellent fellow, incapable of violence, a mathematician, and also very much my friend. Call him in, speak to him frankly, and you will see that he will return to the straight and narrow." [3]

In the second week of November, in an atmosphere thick

[3] Oliveira Vianna, *O Occaso do império*, p. 173.

with rumor and unrest, gossip reported that the President of the Council, to snub the army, had failed to invite its principal representatives to the famous ball on the Ilha Fiscal honoring the visiting Chileans, when as a matter of fact some forty-five received invitations. Another rumor was to the effect that Dom Pedro would abdicate on his next birthday in favor of his daughter. Another was that owing to his mounting infirmities, the Emperor had abandoned the government to associates in the palace, the Princess Imperial and her husband, or to the head of the cabinet, or even to Dom Pedro's private physician, the Conde de Mota Maia.[4] And this impression became general, especially in military circles.

By November 10, the day the infantry embarked for Amazonas, or the day following, the conspiracy was under way, of military officers and republican civilians. The leader among the civilians was Dom Pedro's "friend," Benjamin Constant; among the military as it later appeared, the Adjutant General, Marshal Floriano Peixoto. Many, including Marshal Deodoro da Fonseca, thought that its object was merely to force the resignation or dismissal of the Ouro Preto ministry, but others privately aimed at the overthrow of the monarchy.

It appears that Marshal Deodoro, who was to emerge as nominal leader of the revolution and head of the new regime, long hesitated between the Republic and his respect and friendship for Dom Pedro. At a meeting in his own residence, probably on November 11, the republicans led by Benjamin Constant, and including Rui Barbosa and Quintino Bocaiuva, brought pressure to bear to which he succumbed. He seemingly emerged convinced that "with the monarchy there is no possible salvation for the country or for the Army." [5] Yet it appears that his vacillation persisted after the fall of the min-

---

[4] *Ibid.*, pp. 196–197.
[5] His words on November 12, quoted in Oliveira Vianna, *O Occaso do império*, p. 183.

istry, and almost to the moment of the declaration of the Republic on the afternoon of November 15.[6] The conspirators became apprehensive that their designs would miscarry after all, and at another meeting with Deodoro renewed their assaults upon the impressionable mind of the Marshal. The conclusive argument seems to have been the rumor, skillfully exploited by Benjamin Constant, that the Emperor would call on Senator Silveira Martins of Rio Grande do Sul, a bitter and vindictive enemy of Deodoro, to head the new ministry should the monarchy survive. Self-preservation, escape from the penalties of open rebellion, left no alternative.

When Ouro Preto learned that trouble was brewing among the military, he was reassured by both the Minister of War and Marshal Floriano Peixoto that all was well, although Floriano was deeply involved in the conspiracy. The uprising was apparently set for November 20, the day when the new Parliament was to be installed, but as so often happens in conspiracies against the public order, unforeseen circumstances forced a premature denouement. On the afternoon of November 14, while Ouro Preto was taking emergency measures, calling on the police and the National Guard to stand by, and summoning troops from the province of Rio de Janeiro, the conspirators spread false rumors in the city: various regiments of the garrison were to be scattered at once to the provinces, and Marshal Deodoro and other disaffected generals were to be arrested and rusticated. Early the following morning, when rumors reached the palace grounds, two cavalry regiments and a battalion of infantry at the palace barracks mutinied and marched into the city to the Campo de Sant'Ana, the military headquarters. There the cabinet had already gathered. When after midnight Ouro Preto learned of the mutiny, he had ordered the Marine Arsenal prepared for defense and assembled his ministers there. But Maracajú, the Minister of War, per-

[6] *Ibid.*, pp. 183–189.

suaded them to move to the Army headquarters at the Campo de Sant'Ana to confront the insurgents.

The mutineers arrived at headquarters at about eight o'clock in the morning, accompanied by students from the Military Academy, and surrounded the barracks. The barracks garrison under command of Marshal Floriano, instead of attacking the rebellious troops as Ouro Preto repeatedly ordered, fraternized with them. Marshal Deodoro, who had been ill at home, also arrived, and shortly after informed the cabinet that it was dismissed; but he added, according to Ouro Preto's account, that he intended to ask the Emperor to appoint a new ministry.[7] He then withdrew, leading the insurgents through the streets of the city to the Marine Arsenal, and retired to his own house. It was at this critical juncture, during the morning of the fifteenth, when Deodoro seemed still steadfast in his loyalty to the monarchy, that Benjamin Constant and other republican leaders gathered at his home to overcome his reluctance to coöperate.

Meantime Ouro Preto, during the night and early morning had sent urgent telegrams to the Emperor in Petrópolis, the summer residence, informing him of the course of the rebellion. But for a variety of reasons, chiefly the failure of Dom Pedro to realize the true state of affairs — the Emperor and Empress had been in Rio on the fourteenth when all seemed quiet and peaceful — he was slow in getting under way, and did not arrive in the capital until the early afternoon of the fifteenth. By this time the radical republicans had skillfully taken over the movement, and in the middle of the afternoon

[7] Accounts of events on November 14 and 15 are often conflicting. The best available narrative, based on a wide examination of the sources, is probably that given by M. W. Williams in *Dom Pedro the Magnanimous*, chap. xvii. The story that Marshal Deodoro arrived at the barracks carrying the imperial flag, and that on entering the barracks waved his cap and shouted, "Long live His Majesty the Emperor," has been both affirmed and denied.

the Republic was proclaimed in the City Hall before a large crowd. Somewhat later Marshal Deodoro was announced as head of a new provisional government, with Rui Barbosa as Minister of Finance, Quintino Bocaiuva as Minister of Foreign Affairs, and Benjamin Constant in charge of the War Department. Admiral Wandenkolk, who had welcomed the insurgent column at the Naval Arsenal, remained Minister of Marine. Guards were almost immediately placed about the City Palace, where the imperial family and a few friends were congregated, to preclude their escape, and next morning the sentries were increased to keep anyone from entering or leaving the building.

The group assembled in the palace apparently remained for several hours unaware that the Republic had been proclaimed. In the interval the old Emperor, recoiling from the thought of dictation by the military, at first declined to accept the resignation of the Ouro Preto ministry; and even after acquiescence he stubbornly refused to take positive steps to form a new ministry until early next morning, November 16, in spite of appeals by his family and friends, and even by the Council of State, and then it was too late. It doubtless would have been too late in any case. The plan was to persuade the distinguished and faithful old imperial statesman, Saraiva, to form a government with Deodoro as Minister of War. Saraiva agreed, but Deodoro, already provisional president of the new Republic, was not accessible. Early in the previous evening Ouro Preto and his Minister of Justice, Cândido de Oliveira, had been placed under arrest and held for deportation. It is clear that Dom Pedro from the first had minimized the seriousness of the revolt, refusing to negotiate with the insurgents, and had counted too much on the loyalty of the majority of his subjects.

The question of the disposition of the fallen Emperor was quickly settled. In the afternoon of the sixteenth he and his family received orders to leave Brazil within twenty-four hours. Dom Pedro set two o'clock on the following afternoon as the time of departure. But shortly after midnight came orders from the Provisional Government to embark before daybreak, for fear of popular demonstrations of sympathy for the Emperor and possible violence. The imperial family, accompanied by Dom Pedro's private physician, Mota Maia, and by several close friends who elected to follow them into exile, on a dark and rainy night were put aboard a Brazilian cruiser and carried down the coast to Ilha Grande where they were transferred to the steamer *Alagoas* for banishment to Europe. Before the cruiser left Rio Bay, the provisional authorities agreed to assign 5000 contos to the imperial exiles to cover financial obligations in Brazil and abroad, but Dom Pedro when he learned of it promptly declined to accept the grant. And so for a second time in its history — in 1889 as in 1822 — a radical change was made in the political system of the nation without resort to serious bloodshed.

The Revolution was as much a surprise as had been the abdication of the first Emperor in 1831. "None of the responsible leaders of the two old parties had foreseen an immediate, let alone a violent, end to the old regime. The conviction had been general in all political circles, especially after the law of abolition, that a third reign was unlikely, but all admitted that Dom Pedro would govern to the end." [8] Ouro Preto himself up to the morning of the fourteenth seemed oblivious of the extreme danger he was in; and until surrounded in General Headquarters by the insurgent troops, his orders ignored by Marshal Floriano, he apparently retained confidence in the ultimate fidelity of the army and its officers. Among the latter, especially among older officers who had gained their laurels in the Paraguayan War, there remained a sentiment of gratitude and veneration for the Emperor. Most of the military

[8] Oliveira Vianna, *O Occaso do império*, p. 111.

clique, including Marshal Deodoro, originally aimed at nothing more than a change of ministry. They were maneuvered by Marshal Floriano, and by the republican group dominated by Benjamin Constant, into a thrust against the monarchy itself. Without this band of zealots, the Republic would probably have emerged stillborn. Military discontent gave opportunity to a few ambitious leaders to ape the ways of military dictators in the republics of Spanish America. Ex post facto perspicacity is rarely profitable. It is however interesting to reflect that if Ouro Preto and his cabinet had not sought refuge in the army headquarters, and if Dom Pedro had remained in Petrópolis, the outcome might conceivably have been different. In fact, as early as November 15, before he appeared in Rio, close friends of the Emperor had considered a plan of having him stay in Petrópolis, form a ministry, and govern from there, and if necessary retire farther back into the country, until the nation had time to rally round him.

The Revolution, therefore, was in no sense a popular rising. Except for a few republican leaders, civilians had no active part in it, and in Rio de Janeiro there was no resistance. In the provinces, and in the daily press, there was little serious opposition to the new order established in the capital. Due to a composite of circumstances already reviewed, most of the politically conscious part of the nation seemed stunned or apathetic, even ready to condone the Republic. Most imperial officials at home and abroad, many of whom were personally indebted to Dom Pedro, quickly made terms with the new order. The Emperor had been left in almost complete isolation. The last ministry under the Empire had come in with a program of wide constitutional and financial reform, almost everything that the radicals demanded. But it also faced the vital problem of increasing military insubordination. Except for that it might have saved the monarchy, at least as long as Dom Pedro remained alive. But the ambitions and intrigues of a few military and republican leaders had carried them beyond compromise.

The imperial exiles landed in Lisbon on December 7, and a fortnight later moved on to Coimbra and Oporto, where on the twenty-eighth the Empress died suddenly of a heart attack. Most of the two remaining years Dom Pedro spent at a hotel in Cannes on the Riviera, with visits during the warmer months to his beloved Paris. A month after his departure for Europe, the Provisional Government had issued a decree formally banishing him from Brazil, canceling the imperial civil list as of December 15, and ordering the Braganzas to dispose of all their landed property there within two years. Against this last order Dom Pedro protested, and as a matter of fact the imperial estates remained in possession of the family, and still are insofar as they have not been sold.

From his occupations and diversions in Europe, one would gather that Dom Pedro suffered little of the mental decline of which so much had been made by the opposition before the Revolution. His memory was reported as excellent, and his intellectual interests remained extraordinarily wide. A remarkable linguist, who could read over a dozen languages and speak eight or nine, he continued abroad his studies of Hebrew, Arabic, Sanskrit, and Tupí.[9] He was a voracious reader, attended lectures and concerts, discussed new mathematical formulas with Picard of the French Academy of Sciences, of which he was a foreign associate, carried on a wide correspondence with Brazilian and foreign scholars, and received many visits by Brazilian friends, fellow exiles, and distinguished strangers. But his physical condition could not keep pace with his alertness of mind. His health grew steadily worse, and in Paris an attack of pneumonia proved fatal on December 5, 1891. Dom Pedro and his Empress were entombed in Lisbon among the kings and princes of Portugal.

[9] Williams, *Dom Pedro the Magnanimous*, pp. 250–254, 368.

Thirty years later, in September 1920, when a new generation of Brazilians had grown up strangers to the passions and propaganda of 1889, the decree of banishment was revoked by the National Congress. The bodies of the Emperor and Empress were brought back to Brazil and were placed in a magnificent mausoleum in a church in Petrópolis. And more recently the old imperial residence in Petrópolis has been affectionately restored as a national monument.

Chapter Nine

* * * * * * * * * * * *

THE BALANCE SHEET OF THE EMPIRE

Brazil lived under a monarchy for sixty-seven years, during exactly half of its history to date as an independent state — a unique experience among the nations of America. Canada, it is true, also remained under a monarchy, but its peculiar relationships with the British crown as colony and commonwealth do not constitute a significant parallel. Looking back from the vantage point of 1956 we can discern more clearly the benefits derived by the Brazilian people from this experiment, and also some of the Empire's shortcomings.

To be able to make the transition from a subject, colonial status to political independence without a long and sanguinary military struggle was an inestimable boon, and one vouchsafed to none of Brazil's republican neighbors. Portuguese and Spanish America were moved by the same novel ideological concepts of the time — liberty, equality, democracy — although in both the dominant class, an agrarian aristocracy, equated equality with political, not social, equality, and democracy amid a population mostly illiterate and chiefly Indian or African, with rule by an elite. The revolutionary movement, therefore, although breaking sharply with its traditional, political past, was in most places really conservative. The leaders, mistrusting a genuine democracy, preferred to retain the social molds inherited from old Europe in which they had been formed. This implied a continuing aristocratic society closely allied with the military and the Church, and consolidated under the rule of a prince of royal stature. As we have seen, only for the Brazilians was a prince of their own available, in the heir to the Portuguese crown who for fourteen years had lived among them and loved their country. The transition to independence was therefore relatively easy and quickly accomplished. Open conflict between ultra-conservatives attached to the mother country and the Revolution scarcely appeared in Brazil. In Spanish America it caused a bitter civil war that lasted for a decade and a half. It gave a preponderance to the military element that persisted for several generations and from which some of the Spanish republics have not yet escaped.

The Empire therefore served as a bond between past and present, between the old and the new, the Creole and the Portuguese. It also provided a visible symbol of common, inherited loyalties, not evident in the nascent Spanish republics; held together the widely dispersed provinces and counterbalanced the centrifugal forces that had always been present in Brazilian history. And it insured to the Brazilians an opportunity to learn the first lessons of popular government under a stable and ordered regime. It has often been remarked that without the centripedal influence of monarchy, the vast expanse of Brazil would probably have split up, as did the Spanish territories, into several independent republics. True, Brazil possessed a common language and common literary and religious inheritances. So did Argentina and Chile, Peru and Colombia. But as we have seen, the racial complexion, the climate, and the economic interests of the north, the center, and the south of the long Brazilian seaboard were broadly different, more so than in the Argentine provinces and Chile.

And the consequent divergences in social mores and institutions were as great. Granted that Argentina, Chile, Peru, and Columbia were separated by almost impassable mountains and deserts that made political union impractical, the lack of communications by land between the major areas of the Brazilian litoral created almost as serious an obstacle. The provinces constituted an archipelago of islands between which effective communication was only by sea. And Portuguese America as a group of independent republics would have displayed all the early weaknesses, political and economic, suffered by the nations of Spanish America. That Brazil was able to exert in South America the ascendency she enjoyed in the nineteenth century was due to unity under a strong and respected monarchy.

The advantages promised by the Empire were not always immediately apparent. The temperamental idiosyncrasies of Dom Pedro I hindered rather than helped the development of a national unity and led to his undoing. And in the extreme anarchy that prevailed during the minority of his son was writ large what Brazil might have been as several weak and quarrelsome independent states, the prey of popular demagogues or ambitious military officers. The conservative, propertied classes in Argentina and Peru were powerless to withstand these disruptive forces until well into the second half of the century. Chile, it is true, after a short period of disorders in the 1820's, somewhat analogous to conditions in Brazil during the Regency, because of its social homogeneity emerged as a powerful oligarchy. Colombia, torn between regionalism and centralism, between liberals and clericals, did not obtain political equilibrium until our own time, and very recently suffered the woes of a military dictatorship. In Brazil the propertied class, both conservatives and liberals, sensible of the excesses under the Regency, could rally round the young Emperor as the sole source of national unity and social stability. The monarchy again saved the nation from dismemberment.

The Empire did insure personal liberty and equality before the law. Freedom of the press and of public meeting was secure. It did not, and could not, establish popular government as understood in Anglo-Saxon countries. Nowhere in Latin America, whether republic or empire, was the nation prepared for it. Widespread popular education, free elections, and an enlightened public opinion were essentials. They went together, and the lack of them rendered illusory the fond expectations of political doctrinaires. Whatever constitutions might say, they remained an ideal program for a distant future. Prevailing illiteracy, and in most countries the bulk of the population a semi-servile rural class of Indian or African extraction, made political or military dictatorship, or at best a civilian oligarchy, inevitable. Neither type of government was interested in free elections. Politics were reduced to the struggle of rival, personalist factions within the ruling group; and as a faction once in control of the government was disinclined to withdraw, alternation in office was in Spanish America usually accomplished by violence, by resort to revolution. Nor until recent times was the ruling class greatly interested in the spread of popular education, or in the social amelioration of the submerged part of the population.

Progress in the evolution of constitutional government was therefore extremely slow. It hinged upon the growth of a sense of social responsibility, and of experience in the management of popular forms of political control. This experience is not easily achieved — it is the result of long practice, of much trial and error. Willingness of a minority to accept the decisions of the majority, or of the majority to respect the rights of a minority, although axiomatic, are not self-evident to a politically immature people. The Latin Americans, Portuguese and

Spanish, leaping from royal absolutism to constitutional self-government, started from scratch. And although in the century and a quarter since independence was achieved notable political progress has been made, and constitutional forms are generally observed, it is not wholly surprising that there should be temporary reversions to civilian or military dictatorship, as in Brazil during most of the years between 1930 and 1945, in Colombia recently, and in Venezuela today. Or that Argentina, justly proud of its social and material advance, should experience the complete bankruptcy of party government and fall under the sinister regime of a demagogic Perón. The weakness lay in the unwillingness of oligarchy or popular majority to put public interest before private, a major problem in the evolution of popular government under the best of auspices.

Brazilians, with a similar political and social inheritance from colonial times, labored under all the initial shortcomings of their Spanish American contemporaries. Theirs, too, was a purely agrarian society based upon vast latifundia, worked by African slaves or in the pastoral areas by the illiterate semi-nomad *gaúcho*. Of political experiences in self-government they possessed little that was of profit for the management of an empire, as soon appeared under the first Emperor and the Regency that followed. But by avoiding dangerous experiments, and by preserving for the time being the monarchical framework to which all classes were accustomed, they escaped the major ills of administrative anarchy, military despotism, and periodic revolution with which most of the Spanish republics were afflicted. And by the device of the Moderating Power of the Emperor they evolved at least the semblance of strictly parliamentary government and the assurance of a peaceful rotation of political parties. A highly centralized control was inevitable in any case. The presidential autocracy in Spanish America was in some ways much like a disguised monarchy. But it offered no promise of continued order and regularity, and even less of social and political progress. The Empire afforded to Brazil the political vitality so necessary in the early formative years, long freedom from the specter of militarism, and the discipline and tranquillity to make constitutional government an established and customary procedure.

Some of the fundamental domestic problems, however, remained, which the Empire revealed no great skill in solving. Basically, its social and economic organization was too narrow to support the liberal and progressive structure adumbrated by the Constitution. The dilemma was not peculiar to the Americas. It appeared whenever, after the social cataclysm of the French Revolution, nations embarked upon the experiment of popular, constitutional government. It presented more difficulties in Spanish than in Anglo-America because the former, with a numerous sedentary aboriginal population to exploit, more easily preserved in the New World the aristocratic society and traditions of the Old. In imperial Brazil it was compounded by the prevalence of African slavery. The landed proprietors who ruled the Empire did little or nothing for the promotion of primary or even of secondary education. Although there were several efforts to improve or reform the electoral laws, there never was more than a half-hearted endeavor to render them effective. The *patrão* dictated how his dependents should vote, and the party in control of the administrative machinery saw to it that its candidates always won. With few exceptions the ruling oligarchy refused to face the fact that human slavery was not only morally indefensible but economically disastrous, and only with the greatest reluctance did it finally give way before the insistent popular pressure for abolition. Yet passage from an agrarian to a modern industrial economy was possible only by a transformation of the methods and social system of production.

In Spanish America, whatever the failings of republican government, the ruling class immediately recognized the incompatibility of slavery with political democracy, and the institution was early and more easily eliminated. The liberal revolutions of 1830 and 1848 in Europe made an impact upon society that was less evident in Portuguese Brazil. In the Spanish republics it caused a resurgence of liberal protest against the older, agrarian conservatism that became a landmark in the political evolution of these nations. And in the 1850's the last vestiges of human slavery disappeared. It is true that the large Indian population of the Andean and Central American republics made the question of Negro labor of less importance, and that the vast open spaces and favorable climate of the temperate south early attracted European labor to Argentina and Uruguay. But had it not been for the institution of slavery which relegated manual labor and the mechanic arts to an inferior plane, Brazil, closer to Europe, would much earlier have obtained its quota of European immigration. It was only the extreme south, Rio Grande do Sul and Santa Catarina, and to a lesser degree Paraná, that received any considerable number of colonists from abroad, mostly Germans and Italians. But there the sugar or coffee plantation with its concomitant slavery did not exist, free land was abundant, and the settler became a small, independent farmer producing fruits and grain and other commodities for local consumption.

Imperial society under Dom Pedro II presented many of the pleasing aspects of an agrarian aristocracy enjoying wealth, leisure, social prestige, and the legacy of an ancient culture. This was especially true of the great sugar families of the northeast and the coffee barons of the Rio-Minas-São Paulo triangle. Its retrospective contemplation is always an engaging one for the citizen of an equalitarian democracy. It was a society that produced many distinguished personalities in

public life, orators and statesmen who until the last decade of
the Empire pretty completely dominated the political arena. It
was not a highly intellectual society, resembling in some
respects the wealthy squirearchy of eighteenth-century England. The only scholarly organization of any importance was
the Instituto Histórico e Geográfico Brasileiro, founded in
Rio in 1838 and still running strong; to which should possibly
be added the Law Faculties of Recife and São Paulo, first
established in 1827, as nuclei of higher learning and juridical
culture. The literary contributions of the Empire were not
impressive. There were poets and novelists, most of them
moved by the more romantic aspects of earlier Brazilian times
and reflecting the Indianist preoccupations of the literature
of that age throughout Latin America. But we find their
works generally tedious, and frankly imitative of foreign
models. One composer is remembered today, Carlos Gomes,
whose lyric opera, "O Guarani," is occasionally produced,
more perhaps because of its patriotic appeal than for its artistic
merits. In national architecture there was little achievement of
note. The beautiful churches of Bahia, Pernambuco, and
Minas Gerais had been constructed in the eighteenth century,
Brazilian versions of Portuguese baroque that constitute the
most fascinating architecture of the southern continent, rivaled
only by the churrigueresque of eighteenth-century Mexico.
The Empire produced nothing comparable. The great country
houses, *casas grandes*, surrounded by the *senzalas* of the slaves
and the sugar mills or coffee platforms, are interesting to the
historian as a reflection of the society of another era. But their
bare apartments and room-plan as a rule revealed little archi-
tectural skill or elegance, and by modern standards lacked
comfort and convenience. Domestic urban architecture, when
it departed from the severe simplicity of the early years of the
century, often displayed a tropical luxuriance in which mere
fantasy ran riot.

Whether the conservative, traditionalist forces so conspicuous in Brazilian society in the nineteenth century would have made an earlier or more rapid retreat under a republican system, it is of course impossible to know. Certainly the imperial regime, in spite of the tolerance and open-mindedness of Dom Pedro II, did not encourage rapid social and economic change. The clairvoyant and public-spirited Emperor often seemed a mere voice crying in the wilderness. Nevertheless, Brazil after 1850, in the time of Mauá, was undergoing a slow but significant material transformation. Like the rest of America it began to experience some of the industrial and commercial innovations that were altering the face of western Europe. There was a general increase of wealth and well-being in the upper classes; corporate enterprises, banks and other institutions of credit, were common and private fortunes more numerous. A generally sound national credit abroad assured the inversion of foreign, especially British, capital to supply the deficiency of native capital, build public works and utilities, and maintain the balance of international payments. An urban middle class was emerging that made its presence felt in both the political and the social world. It certainly gave impetus to the abolition movement, and while not the source of the republican agitation, contributed to its spread.

That industrial growth was slow is not remarkable, for Latin America was still primarily a producer of the raw materials of mines and agriculture, and for the time being more profitably and economically imported most of its manufactures from Europe. On the other hand, as reflected in legislation or the lack of it, Parliament controlled by the agrarian interest displayed until the very last years of the Empire little interest in measures designed to encourage native industry and finance. Not until 1888 were adequate laws enacted to promote the organization of limited liability companies. It was left to the Republic to launch the nation upon its modern era of economic enterprise and expansion.

Even in the political sphere the accomplishments of the monarchy were disappointing. Dom Pedro, good "republican" that he was, in his later years showed less interest and initiative in the modernization of the state. And the Princess Isabel, heiress to the throne, although enthusiastically supporting abolition as a moral issue, was in other respects obviously sympathetic with the conservative or reactionary elements in the country. The Empire had made possible a long period of peace and political stability during which the nation became inured to the forms of representative, parliamentary government. But in the political education of the people in the ways of democracy it was apparent that the ruling class had accomplished little. The indifference of the nation at large to the revolutionary change of government imposed upon it in 1889 indicated little awareness of the deep significance of that event. And developments that followed the expulsion of the Emperor soon belied the high hopes and exaggerated optimism of a Rui Barbosa or a Benjamin Constant.[1]

Brazil's first experience with a republic was military dictatorship and civil war. The provisional President, Deodoro da Fonseca, instituted a frankly militarist government: restrictions on the press, generals in control of the provinces, military courts to try conspirators against the Republic. This was perhaps necessary in the beginning, for it had been a revolution by a minority in the capital; even of the army only the Rio garrison had been directly involved. The civilian republicans expected to recover control as soon as things had settled

---

[1] Benjamin Constant died early in 1891, before the former Emperor, embittered by the course of events after the Revolution.

down and a constitution was in operation. But a constituent convention did not meet until a year later, in November 1890, and it was scarcely a democratically elected assembly. The military dictator ordered his governors to draw up lists of obedient and trustworthy electors to choose the provincial deputies. Meantime, however, the provisional regime did accomplish something in the way of reform of the commercial and penal codes and the administration of justice, and in the normalizing of administration.

The new charter of government, promulgated in February 1891, provided for a federal republic of twenty states, with a presidential system like that of the United States, separation of state and Church, and a maximum decentralization of authority. This last innovation was of course no more than a reversion to the regional and particularist tradition that went back to colonial times. The first president and vice-president were elected by the convention, and under pretty obvious pressure from its military members it chose Marshal Deodoro as constitutional President. The vice-president was Marshal Floriano Peixoto.

Under these auspices military rule continued in spite of the Constitution. There was no real autonomy of the so-called sovereign states, and governors were appointed and dismissed at will. The consequence was a rising tide of popular opposition, and a deadlock ensued between President Deodoro and his Congress, which refused to approve the federal budget. This was resolved by the President in characteristic military fashion, by the only way he knew, a presidential *coup d'état.* On November 3, 1891, two decrees were issued, one dissolving the Congress, the other declaring martial law in the Federal District. President Deodoro was again a dictator.

Circumstances economic as well as political accounted for this initial debacle of republican institutions. The revolutionary government in 1889 had immediately embarked on a course of irresponsible extravagance. It raised the pay of all military and naval officers and supplied them and their families with imported goods free of customs duties. It ceded to the Naval Club large properties in the center of Rio "as an insignificant proof of its gratitude for the part it played in the proclamation of the Republic." And the personnel and the budget of all public services at home and abroad were increased. The disappearance of the monarchy also coincided with a period of wild financial speculation. Legislation in the last year of the Empire had facilitated the organization of limited liability companies, and in 1890–91 more corporations were set up than in the whole period of the Empire, many of them for purposes utterly fantastic. The imperial government in 1888–89 had also created a new bank of issue which extended agricultural credits to counteract the effects of Negro emancipation, and it took steps through this bank to put paper on a gold basis. After the Revolution, Rui Barbosa as Minister of Finance extended the right of issue to most banks throughout the country and substituted government bonds for gold as security. All of this was part of a deliberate policy to "sell" the new regime to the nation. The aggregate result was a sharp decline in the exchange value of the milreis, a flight of gold, and in 1891 the inevitable reaction. The fictitious prosperity collapsed.

The response of the nation to the presidential *coup d'état* was immediate. The governor of Pará severed all relations with the federal government until constitutional practice was restored. Within a week Rio Grande do Sul was in full revolt. A fortnight later the Navy joined the opposition and threatened to bombard the city of Rio. The game was up, the temperamental Deodoro resigned, and Vice-President Floriano Peixoto, another militarist, took over. There is some evidence that the revolt, in which both military and civilians were involved, was a conspiracy more militarist than civilian, and that the Vice-President himself may have been involved.

Floriano was of a disposition very different from Deodoro — cool, calculating, apathetic — and his administration started out fairly well. But soon it was perpetuating the worst abuses of its predecessor. Militarism seemed stronger than ever. The political rights of the states were ignored, governors were imposed by military force, and corruption and venality in public service increased. "The violence of the government was equalled only by its vigilance." Espionage was universal. Those who protested were summarily deported, including some of the most distinguished personalities in the country. It was then that Rui Barbosa stood forth as the champion of all the violated liberties and began his vigorous and dramatic career as the brilliant advocate of democracy in Brazil.

The response was another revolt in Rio Grande do Sul in August 1893, demanding the President's resignation, and shortly after the navy again joined. President Floriano however was not intimidated. He took vigorous steps in defense and through the press convinced many that the revolt was a movement to restore the Empire. In this there may have been some truth, for disillusionment regarding the Republic was widespread, especially in the navy. But the navy's increasing jealousy of the army and its privileged position was also a factor in the revolt. There followed a bloody civil war that lasted for eight months, to the ultimate discomfiture of the rebels.

Near the end of the struggle, in March 1894, came the time for the national election. To the surprise of many, President Floriano permitted freedom at the polls, and a civilian candidate, Prudente de Morais Barros, was elected. In the following November, at the time of the transmission of authority, Floriano peaceably surrendered office to the new President. As a matter of fact, he was in failing health and died shortly after. Morais Barros was an eminent lawyer of São Paulo, personally honest and respected by the nation. He had been a prominent member of the old Republican Party in that province, presided over the Constituent Convention, and in 1892 was the candidate for the national presidency of most of the civilian members of the Convention. Under his administration militarism was gradually eliminated from the government (although in 1897 militarists tried to assassinate the President and killed the Minister of War instead). Overt federal interference in state administrations and other abuses of power ceased. Local autonomy was respected, restrictions were removed from the press and from the right of public meeting, and life and property were secure. After the extreme turmoil of the incipient years, Morais Barros and his successors ruled more or less in accord with republican forms — at least until 1930 when the fifteen-year dictatorship of Getúlio Vargas began.

Whether the change from monarchy to republic was of ultimate advantage to Brazil is a fair matter of debate. There was certainly a decline in public morality, increased corruption in public services, and a perennial deficit in public finance. Electoral methods did not improve, and it may be questioned whether a sense of public service, of altruism in public life, is greater than it was in the old political parties under the Empire. Until 1930 Brazil was governed by what was to all intents and purposes an oligarchy, the so-called Republican Party. This was made up of a number of state political machines, each controlled by local family or allied economic interests. Their representatives meeting in caucus nominated a presidential candidate who was invariably elected. The "Party" was dominated in turn by the two wealthiest and most populous states, São Paulo and Minas Gerais, and with two exceptions all the Presidents until 1930 were either Paulistas or Mineiros, chosen alternately. Traces of this former political system still survive, but since the deposition of President Vargas (a native of Rio Grande do Sul) by the army in 1945, elections have more genuinely reflected the popular will. And since 1930 the army, in spite of recent vagaries, has on the whole thrown its weight on the side of democratic government. The isolation of the remote interior is giving way before the radio, and the rural population shows less dependence upon the dictates of the *patrão* or of the local political boss. Although politics in Brazil are often as devious as in many more mature modern democracies, the Republic seems to have entered upon a more authentic, more representative course of development.

There are a few who, moved chiefly by the short-comings of the Republic, still look back with nostalgia to the "good old days" of the Empire. But it is a sentimental regret. There is no monarchical party in Brazil. The clock can never be turned back, nor should it be.

BIBLIOGRAPHY

Abreu, J. Capistrano de. *Ensaios e estudos (crítica e história)*. 3 vols. [Rio de Janeiro], 1931–1938.

Agassiz, Louis. *A Journey to Brazil. By Professor and Mrs. Louis Agassiz*. Boston, 1868.

Armitage, John. *The History of Brazil from the Period of the Arrival of the Braganza Family in 1808 to the Abdication of Dom Pedro the First in 1831*. 2 vols. London, 1836.

Azevedo, Fernando de. *Brazilian Culture*. Tr. William Rex Crawford. New York, 1950.

Azevedo, Vitor de. *Feijó (vida, paixão e morte de um chimango)*. São Paulo, 1942.

Bandeira de Mello, Afonso de Toledo. *O Trabalho servil no Brasil*. Rio de Janeiro, 1936.

Besouchet, Lidia. *Mauá y su época*. Buenos Aires, 1940.

Boehrer, George C. A. *Da Monarquia à república: história do partido republicano do Brasil (1870–1889)*. Tr. Berenice Xavier. [Rio de Janeiro, 1954.]

Box, Pelham H. *The Origins of the Paraguayan War*. 2 vols. Urbana, Illinois, 1927.

Buarque de Holanda, Sérgio. *Raízes do Brasil*. 2nd ed. Rio de Janeiro, 1948.

Calmon, Pedro. *História social do Brasil*. 2 vols. São Paulo, 1937.

Calógeras, João Pandiá. *Formação histórica do Brasil*. 3rd ed. São Paulo, 1938.

——— *O Marquês de Barbacena*. São Paulo, 1932.

——— *A Política exterior do império*. 3 vols. Rio de Janeiro, 1927–1933.

Câmara Cascudo, Luis da. *O Marquês de Olinda e seu tempo (1793–1870)*. São Paulo, 1938.

Castro Carreira, Liberato de. *História financeira e orçamentária do império do Brasil desde a sua fundação*. Rio de Janeiro, 1889.

Castro Rebello, E. de. *Mauá. Restaurando a verdade*. Rio de Janeiro, 1932.

Cardozo, Manoel. "The Holy See and the Question of the Bishop-Elect of Rio, 1833–1839," *The Americas*, X, 3–74.

Corrêa da Costa, Sérgio. *As Quatro corôas de D. Pedro I*. [São Paulo, 1941].

Cunha, Euclides da. *A Margem da história*. 3rd ed. Porto, 1922.

Diégues Junior, Manuel. *Etnias e culturas no Brasil*. Rio de Janeiro, 1952.

Dornas Filho, João. *O Padroado e a igreja brasileira*. São Paulo, [1938].

Ellis Junior, Alfredo. *Feijó e a primeira metade do século XIX*. São Paulo, 1940.

Ewbank, Thomas. *Life in Brazil; or, A Journal of a Visit to the Land of the Cocoa and the Palm*. New York, 1856.

Faria, Alberto de. *Irenêo Evangelista de Sousa, Barão e Visconde de Mauá, 1813–1889*. 2nd ed. São Paulo, 1933.

Fleiuss, Max, and others. *Contribuições para a biografia de D. Pedro II*. Part I. (Special volume of the Revista do Instituto histórico e geográfico brasileiro.) Rio de Janeiro, 1925.

Freyre, Gilberto. *Casa-grande e senzala*. 2 vols. 5th ed. Rio de Janeiro, 1946.

—— *Nordeste*. Rio de Janeiro, 1937.

—— *Sobrados e mucambos*. São Paulo, 1936.

Goulart, Maurício. *Escravidão africana no Brasil (Das origens à extinção do tráfico)*. 2nd ed. São Paulo, [1950].

Kidder, D. P., and J. C. Fletcher. *Brazil and the Brazilians, Portrayed in Historical and Descriptive Sketches*. Philadelphia, 1857.

Koster, Henry. *Travels in Brazil*. London, 1816.

Lacombe, Américo Jacobina. *Brasil: período nacional*. (Inst. Panamer. Geog. Hist., Comisión de Historia, Programa de Historia de América, III, 1.) Mexico, 1956.

Lima Barbosa, Mário de. *Ruy Barbosa*. São Paulo, [1949].

Lyra, Heitor. *História de D. Pedro II*. 3 vols. São Paulo, 1938–1940.

Magalhães, Basílio. *Estudos de história do Brasil*. São Paulo, 1940.

Manchester, Alan K. *British Preëminence in Brazil, Its Rise and Decline: A Study in European Expansion*. Chapel Hill, 1933.

Martin, Percy Alvin. "Causes of the Collapse of the Brazilian Empire," *Hisp. Amer. Hist. Review*, IV, 4–48.

—— "Slavery and Abolition in Brazil," *Hisp. Amer. Hist. Review*, XIII, 151–196.

Mauá, Irinêo Evangelista de Souza, Visconde de. *Autobiografia (exposição aos credores e ao público)*. Edição prefaciada e anotada por Claudio Ganns. Rio de Janeiro, 1942.

—— *Correspondência política de Mauá no Rio da Prata (1850–1885)*. Prefácio e notas de Lidia Besouchet. São Paulo, 1943.

Monteiro, Tobias de Rêgo. *História do império: a elaboração da independência.* Rio de Janeiro, 1927.

—— *História do império: o primeiro reinado.* 2 vols. Rio de Janeiro, 1939.

Nabuco, Carolina. *A Vida de Joaquim Nabuco.* 3rd ed. São Paulo, 1943.

Nabuco, Joaquim. *Um Estadista do império: Nabuco de Araujo, sua vida, suas opiniões, sua época.* 3 vols. Rio de Janeiro, [1897].

Normano, J. F. *Brazil: A Study of Economic Types.* Chapel Hill, 1935.

Octavio, Rodrigo. *Minhas memórias dos outros.* 3 vols. Rio de Janeiro, 1934–1936.

Oliveira Lima, Manuel de. *Formation historique de la nationalité brésilienne.* Paris, 1911.

—— *O Império brasileiro, 1822–1889.* São Paulo, [1927].

—— *O Movimento da independência, 1821–1822.* São Paulo, 1922.

—— *Dom João VI no Brasil, 1808–1821.* 2 vols. Rio de Janeiro, 1908.

Oliveira Vianna, F. J. *Evolução do povo brasileiro.* 2nd ed. São Paulo, 1933.

—— *O Occaso do império.* 2nd ed. São Paulo, [1933].

Ortigão, Ramalho. *A Moeda circulante do Brasil.* Rio de Janeiro, 1914.

Ouro Preto, Afonso Celso de Assis Figueiredo, Visconde de. *Oito annos de parlamento (1881–1889).* 2nd ed. São Paulo, [1928].

Prado Junior, Caio. *História econômica do Brasil.* São Paulo, 1945.

Rangel, Alberto. *Gastão de Orléans, o último Conde d'Eu.* São Paulo, 1935.

—— *D. Pedro I e a Marquesa de Santos.* São Paulo, 1916.

Santos, José Maria dos. *A Política geral do Brasil.* São Paulo, 1930.

Sousa, Octavio Tarquinio de. *Bernardo Pereira de Vasconcellos e seu tempo.* Rio de Janeiro, 1937.

—— *Diogo Antônio Feijó (1784–1843).* Rio de Janeiro, 1942.

—— *História de dois golpes de estado.* Rio de Janeiro, 1939.

—— *José Bonifacio, emancipador del Brasil.* Mexico, 1945.

—— *A Vida de D. Pedro I.* 3 vols. São Paulo, 1952.

Spalding, Walter. *A Revolução farroupilha.* São Paulo, 1939.

Stein, Stanley J. "The Passing of the Coffee Plantation in the Paraíba Valley," *Hisp. Amer. Hist. Review,* XXXIII, 331–364.

—— *Vassouras. A Brazilian Coffee County, 1850–1900.* Cambridge, Mass., 1957.

Taunay, Afonso de E. *A Missão artística de 1816.* (Publ. da Diretoria do patrimônio hist. e artist. nacional, no. 18.) Rio de Janeiro, 1956.

Valladão, Alfredo. *Da Acclamação à maioridade, 1822–1840.* São Paulo, 1934.

Vianna, Helio. *Estudos de história imperial.* São Paulo, 1950.

Vianna Filho, Luiz. *A Vida de Rui Barbosa.* São Paulo, 1952.

Vilhena de Moraes, E. *Novos aspectos da figura de Caxias.* Rio de Janeiro, 1937.

Walsh, R. *Notices of Brazil in 1828 and 1829.* 2 vols. London, 1830.

Williams, Mary Wilhelmine. *Dom Pedro the Magnanimous.* Chapel Hill, 1937.

INDEX

Aberdeen Act, 91

Additional Act of 1834, 51, 58

African slave trade. *See* Slave trade

Almeida Martins, Father, 117

Amelia of Leuchtenberg, Empress of Brazil, 38, 40

Andrada, Antônio Carlos de: and anti-Portuguese demonstrations, 25; exiled to Europe, 28; returns to Brazil, 39; leads the *maioristas*, 53–54; heads ministry, 54, 57

Andrada, José Bonifácio de: early career, 16; chief minister of D. Pedro, 16, 20; and the National Assembly, 24, 25; his character, 26; banished to Europe, 28; returns to Brazil, 39; tutor of Pedro II, 42; name associated with *restauradores*, 50

Andrada, Martim Francisco de: and anti-Portuguese demonstrations, 25; Minister of Finance, 25, 27; exiled to Europe, 28; returns to Brazil, 39; member of ministry, 54

Antonelli, Giacomo, Cardinal, 121, 124

Araújo Lima, Pedro de. *See* Olinda, Pedro de Araújo Lima, Marquês de

Argentina: sentiment for monarchy in, 1, 2; compared with Brazil, 3n, 158, 159; conflict with Brazil over the Banda Oriental, 10, 34–35, 72; and Río de la Plata politics, 73–81 *passim*

Army, the: Pedro I and, 46, 127–128; mutinies during the Regency, 46, 128; in Paraguayan War, 80–81, 129; Pedro II and, 128, 130, 148; republicanism in, 129; increasing indiscipline of, 131–134, 141–142, 147–148; conspiracy against the Crown, 149–152; and democracy, 171

Aurora Fluminense, 45

Banda Oriental: conflict with Argentina over, 10, 34–35, 72; Portuguese expelled from, 21–22

Banks, 36, 65, 104, 168

Barbacena, Felisberto Brant Pontes, Marquês de, 40, 41

Barbosa, Rui: Minister of Finance under the Republic, 104, 152, 168; standard bearer of liberalism, 139, 169; associated with the republicans, 146, 149, 166

Benjamin Constant. *See* Botelho de Magalhães, Benjamin Constant

Beresford, William Carr Beresford, Viscount, 10, 12

Bocaiuva, Quintinio, 139, 149, 152

Botelho de Magalhães, Benjamin Constant: tutor of Emperor's grandchildren, 138; republican leader, 139; disciple of Auguste Comte, 139; attacks the government, 148; in conspiracy against the monarchy, 149, 150, 151, 154; Minister of War, 152; death of, 166n

Brazil: compared with Spanish America, 2, 3, 4, 23, 60, 157–163 *passim*, with Portugal, 3, with the United States, 3, 162; growth of nationalistic sentiment in, 3–4; effects of presence of the Crown on, 5–9; race relations, 8–9; legal equality with Portugal, 9–10; and the Río de la Plata, 10, 34–35, 72–